A
PARENT'S GUIDE
FOR
SUICIDAL
AND
DEPRESSED
TEENS

A PARENT'S GUIDE FOR SUICIDAL AND DEPRESSED TEENS

Help for Recognizing if a Child is in Crisis and What to Do About It

KATE WILLIAMS

HAZELDEN®

Hazelden
Center City, Minnesota 55012-0176

Library of Congress Cataloging-in-Publication Data
Williams, Kate.
    A parent's guide for suicidal and depressed teens : help for recogniz-
ing if a child is in crisis and what to do about / Kate Williams.
        p.   cm.
    Includes bibliographical references.
    ISBN 1-56838-040-2 : $11.95 ($17.95 Can.)
    1. Youth—Suicidal behavior. 2. Parent and teenager. 3.
Suicide—Prevention. 4. Adolescent psychology.   I. Title.
HV6546.W55 1995
362.28'0835—dc20   94-46390
                                                            CIP

Editor's note
Hazelden offers a variety of information on chemical dependency and related areas. Our publications do not necessarily represent Hazelden's programs, nor do they officially speak for any Twelve Step organization.

The writings of Jill Breckenridge, Rachel Firchow, Mary B. Kahle, Bernie
Schemmler, Richard Solly, Rachel W., Cary Waterman, and Linda Wing are
published by the generous permission of the authors.

Adult Children of Alcoholics, also known as *The Laundry List,* by Tony A., was
previously published in *The Laundry List: The ACOA Experience.* Reprinted
by the generous permission of Tony A.

A Message to Teenagers . . . How to tell when drinking is becoming a problem
is reprinted with permission of Alcoholics Anonymous World Services, Inc.
Permission to reprint these questions does not mean that AA has reviewed
or approved the contents of this publication nor that AA agrees with the
views expressed herein.

Your Lifestyle Profile was developed for community service by the Allstate
Insurance Companies and reprinted with their kind permission.

The author wishes to express her gratitude to all the writers whose words
have supported her recovery and her work.

If suffering alone taught, all the world would be wise, since everyone suffers. To suffering must be added mourning, understanding, patience, love, openness, and the willingness to remain vulnerable.

—ANNE MORROW LINDBERGH

Contents

Contents

Foreword

By Denise M. D'Aurora, M.Ed.

When I was approached about writing the foreword to *A Parent's Guide for Suicidal and Depressed Teens* I did not know that the book was written from Ms. Williams' experience as a parent whose child was both depressed and suicidal. As a family therapist, I was increasingly gratified to find as I read the book that the author offered genuine insight into the treatment of depressed adolescents and practical help for families in crisis.

I was interested in reading the book for many reasons. Chief among these is that I encourage and suggest reading to my clients as an adjunct to therapy and am always looking for quality books to recommend. Although there is no dearth of personal growth literature available, much of it is unremarkable. Kate Williams' book is an enormous exception to this.

As Ms. Williams states, "Books about depression and suicide. . . tend to be clinical and descriptive. They tend to talk about 'clients'. . . the advice tends to be unusually vague, like 'Listen.'" Her own needs as a parent were for support, for information offered at a level sensitive to her feelings, and for information about the experience of other parents in a similar situation. She found no book that addressed all of her needs. However, out of the recognition that her needs were not unique, after reflection on her own experience, and with both courage and generosity in sharing that experience, she has written a book that will be of great value to parents in this difficult and painful situation.

My own work as a family therapist has taught me that like Ms. Williams, most parents are terrified by the knowledge that their child is seriously depressed and may be thinking about suicide. Most of the parents I have worked with have felt shamed or felt that their feelings are invalid in some way—rather than supported in their own pain and recognized as important partners in their child's treatment and recovery. The negative messages can and sometimes do come from the attitudes and demeanor of professionals involved in treatment. Ms. Williams details some of the insensitivities that those of us who work with families all too often commit. It is my hope that her comments will serve as wake-up calls for all of us professionals.

As Kate Williams notes, other parents may make negative comments about a family in this painful situation out of their own fear. It is human nature to desire a certain amount of distance, physical or emotional, between ourselves and a painful reality. A family with a child who is depressed, suicidal, or in treatment is often a terrifying reminder to the network of families around it. Needing to reassure themselves that their own children are okay, these other families may make thoughtless comments or cut off contact with the parent or family in crisis, rather than offer the supportive, nurturing attention that family needs.

One important service that this book provides is an account of one parent's process that can validate the experience of others in similar circumstances. Additionally, it offers insights to those who are in proximity to these parents, suggesting ways to be caring resources rather than sources of more pain.

Ms. Williams also explores many of the underlying developmental and specific situational components in adolescent depression—never in a way that extends to advice giving or judgment— but as opportunities for further work toward full recovery for the adolescent, the parent, and the family. Her penetrating comments on what she terms the *Romance of Death* in our culture and its particular impact on vulnerable adolescents, for example, raise questions for all of us as parents, educators, and consumers. These questions require serious consideration and clear statements to our children about our own values about life and the opportunities that it presents along with the pain that sometimes comes with living in our world.

She addresses sexuality as a topic to be talked about in a forthright manner—whether the questions are about sexual activity, sexual orientation, or the murky business of defining for oneself just what constitutes masculinity or femininity.

As professionals, we have insufficiently described the specific developmental concerns faced by adopted children and their families. Again, Ms. Williams is neither prescriptive nor judgmental in her comments but encourages families to openly and honestly define what this particular life experience means for their children, including how their needs at adolescence may differ from those of their peers.

In looking at these areas, Ms. Williams presents her own journey and what has worked for her and for her daughter in a way that is optimistic and hopeful without minimizing the hard work and painful searching involved. She has literally opened her experience to others in a very honest, generous way with neither apologies nor self-recrimination. She describes her own therapeutic work and how the threads of her own life weave in and out of her daughter's recovery without the assumption that she could control that recovery or the assumption of blame for the illness itself. This role is the most useful, responsible, and healthy perspective for parents to arrive at in the course of a family crisis like this one, and it requires the development of a balance between hard work and self-care that Ms. Williams promotes time and again in the first two parts of this book and returns to in the final section.

I will confidently recommend this book to families that I work with and suggest it as well to those of us who walk with them as professionals and friends.

DENISE M. D'AURORA, M.ED.
Licensed Psychologist
Licensed Marriage and Family Therapist
Family Therapy Institute, Inc.
St. Paul, Minnesota

Introduction

My daughter Rachel suddenly—it seemed—didn't want to live. At the time she was thirteen and in the eighth grade. We started going to a therapist immediately, both together and separately. This went on for two years. Then, after Christmas vacation in tenth grade, she had a nervous breakdown. I know *nervous breakdown* is an old-fashioned term that really isn't used much anymore, but it is the best word to describe what happened. Rachel couldn't stop crying, she couldn't get off the couch, she didn't know what was wrong, and she said she couldn't think of any reason she wanted to live.

Then I found a different therapist, Barbara. After meeting with Rachel two times, the therapist met with me and my daughter and said she was concerned about her. "Concerned about your daughter." Those calm words struck terror in my heart. The three of us decided together that Rachel needed the physical security of a hospital. She stayed in an adolescent crisis unit for ten days and then entered a daytime mental health program, living at home. She continued to work with Barbara.

After a shaky reentry to regular life, she went back to her high school. She has now graduated from high school, after continuing to work on her issues for five years. We continue to go to therapy, working on both our personal and family issues.

This book is a brief summary of the past five years, a time of incredible pain and change. We have not come to the end of the story, however. Rachel is going to have a lifelong task of managing her mood swings and living in a healthy way that nurtures her and keeps her on a level course. She will probably continue to be challenged by issues of abandonment and dependency. My task is to learn how to support her, to stay out of her way, to set limits, and to continue to learn how to have a "normal" family life.

During the past five years, I've received help from many people with this difficult situation. Most helpful have been Rachel's therapist, Barbara; my sister; and my friends.

What I *didn't* find was a book that spoke to me as a parent. There are many books about depression and suicide, but they tend to be clinical and descriptive. They tend to talk about "clients," a manner of speaking that has never felt supportive to me. Or they talk about what was wrong with the clients' families without saying what could be righted in a "wrong" situation. If a book does speak to parents, the advice tends to be unusually vague, like "Listen." Fortunately, there was one book, *Suicide: The Forever Decision: For Those Thinking*

About Suicide, and For Those Who Know, Love, and Counsel Them, that was a lifesaver in teaching me how to talk about suicide.

But I longed to read a book that would tell me how other parents have dealt with this situation. I wanted a book I could connect with on a feeling level. It wasn't there. So I'm writing the book I wanted to read. I have tried to include resources, encouragement, and suggestions for a path of action for parents in a similar situation. I've organized the book according to the order of the changes I went through. But I hope other parents will feel free to skip around in the book if their journeys take different turns.

I'm writing this book pseudonymously for three reasons. The first reason is to protect my daughter's identity. When she is an adult, she may want to write her own story about her experience with mental health issues. I don't want to make that decision for her, even though she has given me her consent to write about her and even though some of her writing is included in this book. The second reason is to protect my anonymity as a member of Alcoholics Anonymous and Al-Anon. One of the traditions of Twelve Step programs is that we remain anonymous in the press in order to protect both ourselves and the organization. To tell the story of my life as a mother, I need to write openly about the Twelve Steps, and I can't be as open as I want to be if my real name is published. I believe this book will be more useful to others because I am open about my alcoholism and recovery. The third reason for using a pseudonym is to write freely without fear of being sued by Rachel's father who continues to deny she has any problems.

As I wrote this book, I changed the names of all the people and certain details to protect the anonymity of my family. And, in some cases, I summarized events to a great extent. Sometimes I've been confused about the order that things happened. But all the events I describe happened; all the people in the book are real people in my life.

I have chosen to use the word *child* and *children* throughout the book, even though the child I refer to is now eighteen years old, taller than I am, and more stylishly attired. Why the word *child?* No matter how old our children become, they are still our children. When we see their grown-up bodies, we also see their first wobbly steps, their fine baby hair, the moment they found their balance on a two-wheeled bike. When we see our children we see their history—and ours. We see all the hopes we've had for them along the way. When I see the word *adolescent,* I don't see hope, I see a psychology textbook, so I've used that word less often. When I see the word *teenager,* I'm reminded of commercialism and brand-name blue jeans. So when I use the word *child,* I am affirming the hope we have had for them and the hope we must continue to hold: the hope that they will be able to live a good life.

I know that there must be many people out there who have also looked for support through books because teenage suicide continues to rise. It is the second highest cause of death for teenagers, following accidents. Many deaths called accidents may be suicides. One recent study reports that 34 percent of high school students have thought of suicide recently, and 14 percent have tried.[1] The actual numbers are even higher among American Indians, other young people of color, and lesbian and gay adolescents.[2] When I think of these statistics, I am still shocked, even after five years of work. But I no longer am numb in disbelief.

My heart goes out to all those kids who are looking for a reason to live. And my heart goes out to all you parents who are stunned to discover the extent of your children's pain. I believe that there is a path through the pain, for those on both sides of the generations. Yet I wrote this book for other parents, *not* for children. The idea here is that when we as parents get healthier, we can help our children. Do not give this book to your child! Read it and do your own homework.

I hope that telling my story will help others find hope for themselves and their children.

Part One

Recognizing the Crisis

I have nothing to live for.
—RACHEL

1

The Downward Spiral: Recognizing a Cry for Help

> . . . how frightening it is for her
> to let go of this cloak and embrace life.
> —BETH K. COHEN

My daughter was in trouble and I didn't recognize the signs. She was wearing black clothes, reading poetry about death by Anne Sexton and Sylvia Plath. She was reading a teenage novel about girls who liked to read depressing women poets. They were cool. She liked to sit in her room with the shades pulled, listening to music by candlelight. On the other hand, she had a new boyfriend who looked like a nice kid—he even liked the Beatles! They spent a lot of time taking walks at twilight and wrestling and rolling around in the fall leaves.

On some levels, her behavior seemed typical for an eighth grader. I work part-time as a writer and part-time as a teacher, and I know many kids in the eighth grade classes I teach who fall in love with the color black, who wear black fingernail polish and heavy metal T-shirts with macabre drawings on them. The hormone storm of adolescence stirs up thoughts and fears about growing up, sadness over childhood losses, and a new sense of mortality. Sometimes it seems like all teenagers are thinking, "If my body can erupt like this and turn my feet into size-10 monsters, why couldn't I drop dead at any minute also?"

But even though Rachel seemed typical, we were having problems at home. My second husband and I had split up during the previous summer. Because of the impending divorce, I was under financial and emotional stress.

Yet I thought I was in a good place to handle these changes. I had been through a difficult time and had made big changes in my life. In the previous five years, I had dealt with some difficult issues: sexual abuse in my childhood, physical abuse by Rachel's dad, my second husband's drinking, and my own alcoholism. To make a long story short, I had sobered up, gone to therapy, and now felt optimistic about life. I had a sense of resolution about my family of origin. I thought I was done with serious issues for a while. I thought I was due for a breather. I got about three weeks.

I couldn't afford to keep up our big old house myself. Rachel and I agreed to sell the house rather than take in roommates, but when it was time to put the house on the market, her feelings of loss came up strongly. "Mom," she said, "you're selling my childhood." I felt like a failure being this old and this poor. I felt like a failure being twice-divorced. And yet I was hopeful. Even though I was angry, I believed in the promises of the Twelve Step program. I thought we had hit bottom as a family and would be on the way up as soon as we got relocated. The change in atmosphere would be, I thought, positive.

Because of all the positive changes—the lack of marriage problems and my hope for recovery—I didn't expect my daughter to continue to act out. It's as though I were hoping that she would never have to rebel against me. But rebellion is a normal part of a child's separation from his or her parents, no matter whether the parents have been married for twenty-five years or divorced four times. Even when a family is healthy, rebellion is a normal part of growing up.

Welcome Crisis-Intervention

In the years since, I have found out that what happened is common in early recovery: I was finally living in a stable, trustworthy way, and my daughter unconsciously knew it was safe for her to get the attention she needed for her problems. I could be there for her in a way that I was not capable of before.

The school social worker called me one morning and said, "We have Rachel here in the office and she's having a problem. We want you to come up to school." As I was soon to learn, the problem was twofold: Rachel feared she was pregnant, and the school counselor feared she was at risk for suicide.

I told the social worker my car was in the shop but I could walk there in fifteen minutes. She apparently didn't think that was fast enough because she offered to come and pick me up. My mind flooded with fear. What could it be? If she were sick, they would've called an ambulance. If she were using drugs, there wouldn't be this rush.

I had no idea they were going to tell me they considered her at risk for suicide. I didn't see the warning signs. When Rachel had started reading Anne Sexton, I was pleased because she had hardly ever wanted to read books. I didn't know she was becoming preoccupied with dying, with Anne Sexton's suicide. I didn't see how depressed and stressed she was. Selling the house, the divorce, and the loss of her stepfather were significant changes for her. And there were other things that were putting her under stress that nobody recognized until much later. I am not saying that the divorce caused her to be suicidal, but the divorce was a trigger.

Acting Out: The Separation Process

It's often hard to differentiate between what is normal teen rebellion for the sake of separation and what is over the line. For instance, lots of kids wear black clothes and black lipstick. When adolescents separate from the family unit, they need to experiment with many styles of dress and manners in order to discover which suits them the best. Within any one high school, there may be a multitude of different looks. Yet even as they defiantly go out the door in their ripped jeans, they may feel out on a limb. Separating is lonely. They may have other feelings attached to the loneliness: shame, loss, isolation, anger. They may be mad they have to grow up. In any case, defiance expressed in clothing and appearance is not in and of itself an indication of suicidal tendencies.

Pay Attention to the Warning Signs

Below is a typical list of warning signs exhibited by teens at risk for suicide.[1] Those signs with an asterisk (*) are the most telling. Remember, reading such a "list" should only be used as a first step. We need to add in our own observations and opinions about what spells danger for our kids.

13

Warning Signs . . .

- Talk of killing themselves, as if there is no hope.
- A change in friends or the amount of time spent with friends.
- Sudden change in behavior.*
- Dramatic change in appetite.
- Sleeping difficulties (and too much sleeping).
- Problems at school.
- Inability to concentrate or sit still.
- Confused thought processes; inability to "think straight."
- Unexplained loss of energy (or wild variations in energy levels).
- Increased drug/alcohol use.*
- Constant feeling of worthlessness or self-hatred (may be covered up).
- Excessive risk-taking (driving recklessly, alcohol use, sex without contraception).*
- Misuse of sex and physical relationships.
- Preoccupation with death, dying, or suicide.*
- Giving away personal or prized possessions.*
- Family history of depression and suicide.

This list is so broad that it may apply to all teenagers at one time or another. I think it's hard to interpret something like "sudden change in behavior." My daughter was only showing up as at risk with one item on this list. Consequently, I'd suggest that even if there's only one warning sign, you should pay attention to it and pursue the subject more directly. For example, the primary warning sign my daughter gave was her preoccupation with death and books and movies about people in love with death. I didn't know how to ask her what it meant. I didn't know how to address the preoccupation directly. I needed the help from a therapist to be able to say, "Do you want to die?" and "Do you have a plan?"

Later I found out she was having school problems. Then I found out she was also taking physical risks, for example, literally walking out into traffic. And much later, we found her biological family history, which includes suicide and depression— information the courts withheld from my husband and me when we adopted Rachel shortly after her birth. But I knew none of this at the time. Eventually I had to let go of wishing I'd caught on sooner. I'm grateful I found out before it was too late. I'm grateful somebody noticed the warning signs.

Many checklists note that if three or four factors are present, suicide is possible. I'd like to reiterate that if you even see one risk factor, if you have the slightest flutter of fear that your child is in danger, take action. Don't wait to see four problems manifested.

The writers of the flyer *Help During a Fragile Time* suggest that there are four especially serious signals:

1. Threats or talk of killing themselves.

2. Preparing for death evidenced by giving away prized possessions, making a will, writing farewell letters, gathering pills, or saying good-bye.
3. Talking as if there is no hope, even in the future.
4. Acting or talking as if not a single person cares; completely giving up on themselves and others.

I think that number 4 is especially significant for me, because when I look back I can remember Rachel saying, "Nobody cares." I couldn't believe she really felt that way, so I didn't let the words sink in. After all, I cared so much! How could she not know I cared?

If you are reading this and wondering if your child is in trouble, take time to seriously consider each warning sign. Let your defenses down and think about what you child *actually* says to you, not what you think is true.

However you receive the warning that your child is in danger, your first responsibility is to get help immediately. You need to let your child know you care, even if you are scared and horrified. You need to say directly, "I love you and I don't want you to die. I want you to live. I want you to find a way to have some hope." You don't need to worry about "putting an idea" in your child's mind. Ideas about suicide permeate the youth culture. Be direct.

The next thing to say, over and over until your child has heard you is "Whatever problem you have, there is a solution. We will find a way to solve your problems. *There has to be a way to let go of some of this pain.*"

Insist on Getting Professional Help

Many teenagers are ferociously opinionated about counselors. Nonetheless, it is important to find a way to convince your child to get help. You can say, "If you had a broken leg, I wouldn't let you sit here, and I think your unhappiness is just as serious as a broken leg."

To find help, you can call information and ask for the number of any crisis hot line, which can refer you to a suicide hot line. Or you can call any of the following people and ask them to recommend a therapist: the school counselor, principal, teacher or social worker; your pastor, priest, or rabbi; your doctor. Keep calling until you find someone.

Whatever you do, don't minimize or ignore your child's statement about wanting to die. And don't ever "call their bluff," even in a joking way. A person who says he or she wants to die is in some kind of pain, and it is not up to us to judge the severity of that pain. Also, don't be put off if your child suddenly retracts a suicidal comment by saying, "I was only kidding." You should follow up, especially if there is another warning sign.

2

The Grim Reaper:
Looking at Your Own Feelings

> Children awaken your own sense
> of self when you see them
> hurting, struggling, testing;
> when you watch their eyes and
> listen to their hearts. Children
> are gifts, if we accept them.
> —KATHLEEN TIERNEY CRILLY

The day the school social worker called me into her office to discuss her increasing concern about Rachel, I took my daughter to Planned Parenthood and set up an appointment with one of the family therapists at our health maintenance organization (HMO). My reaction to the crisis about a possible pregnancy was calm, but my emotional reaction to her thinking about suicide was horror.

I wasn't overly angry about the chance of pregnancy because I could account for it psychologically. Rachel was dependent on her boyfriend; her stepfather had left us without a word; and her father was busy being a workaholic doctor who gave her lots of loving words but little time or money. This combination of positive and negative behavior can be crazy-making. Her early sexual behavior seemed to fit with working out her feelings about men, abandonment, and searching for belonging. But I was terribly sad. I could understand it, but it made me feel guilty and sad that my choices had been such that Rachel hadn't had a stable father-figure in her life.

When I took Rachel to the doctor for birth control pills a few days after the pregnancy test at Planned Parenthood, I cried when I heard the nurses saying, "She's only thirteen." I'd told her many times before that I didn't think thirteen was old enough to have a sexual relationship. But it was obvious that this early sexuality was happening with many girls at her school. So I supported her. It was my responsibility to help her get birth control because I believed she had decided to be sexual regardless of what anyone said.

If your child has become sexually active, you must sort through your feelings so that you are able to be actively supportive.

Learn to Talk about Death Calmly

As I said before, I was terrified by the possibility of suicide. But when your child is talking about death and wanting to die, you have to learn how to talk about suicide in a calm manner. For me the first step in being a responsible parent in this situation was working through my feelings on the subject. As I mentioned earlier, the book *Suicide: The Forever Decision* helped me to talk directly about suicide, and that reduced my panic and terror.

If your child is talking about suicide, you are probably having intense feelings, including fear, anger, sadness, shame, and panic. I've been there, I know how intense it is, and I want you to know you can get through this time of fear. But to get through it, you have to let yourself feel the feelings.

I've divided the rest of this chapter into sections on different feelings and responses. Skip around to what seems most applicable to your life. Later I'll suggest ways to deal with these responses.

Denial

I don't know if denial is really a feeling. I think it is a block against any feeling, a lack of feeling, the refusal to feel the fear and anger and sadness at the possibility that your child could be contemplating suicide. But I call it a feeling because it's on a checklist of feelings I measure myself against every so often. Am I facing reality? Am I pretending everything is wonderful even though my daughter is lying on the couch watching TV with no desire to call a friend? I need to check out my denial rating often.

Panic

My first reaction to the idea of suicide was panic. I couldn't accept it. My mind flooded with a white light that was like electricity short-circuiting my thoughts. How could she not want to live? This beautiful person who had been such an incredibly alive baby and toddler! This was so impossible!

Panic is just a short step from denial. When I was feeling panicky, I said to myself, "Calm down. Why is this so hard for you?" I traced my panic to many factors: fear, stress, grief, and regret. I also attribute panic to my lack of information about suicide. But nobody else seemed to know much either. I often thought I was in over my head.

Fear

All parents fear losing their children, some probably more than others. This is a normal fear. We have put so much energy into their lives. Whether we've been "good" or "bad" parents, all of us have given much. The process of raising children makes us attached to them, whether our relationship is smooth or stormy. We are attached and involved.

At the time I think my fear was more intense because I'd lost my younger brother to an overdose when he was twenty. Nobody knows if his death was a suicide. The grief over this loss has often made me fearful and overprotective of my love relationships. I've heard it said that after the first death there is no other. That is true, but it may also be said that after the first death, you want there to be no other.

I had to grieve the loss of my brother in order to keep the fear of death from controlling my behavior with my daughter. In the process of this work, I discovered that she had romanticized my brother's death. She saw death as a hippie heaven where people sit around in the clouds drinking tea and listening to Cat Stevens. I shuddered to think that this fantasy had descended down the generations, that the true cause of his death had become a family secret. I was the only one in my family willing to talk about his life and death. The rest of them remained silent.

A year into Rachel's and my work in therapy I told her, "You may think I miss my brother and that's true. I never get over missing him. But I'm also mad at him. I'm mad because he left me. He was the one person in the family most like me. I'll never stop missing him because he's not here. And if you choose to die I will not romanticize your life, I'll be pissed."

Take some quiet time and ask yourself about your fear of death. What experiences have you had with death that may add a charge to your present fear?

Anger

My anger at the idea of losing Rachel feels healthy because I can express and release it. But often anger is like a shotgun feeling—when we're angry we may not know what it's all about. You may be angry at an ex-spouse who hasn't supported your child. You may be angry at the "system." You may be angry at your suicidal son or daughter for scaring you.

If you're walking around angry at everything without expressing, focusing, and releasing these feelings, anger is going to prevent you from dealing appropriately with your child's pain. When you're angry you need to explore the other feelings that are linked to it and *feel them,* then deal with each issue one by one so the anger doesn't block your response to other events in your life.

Fear of Failure: Shame

Parents of suicidal teens suffer a double-dose of shameful feelings. On the one hand, much of our sense of self-esteem is connected to the idea of being good parents. On the other hand, suicide is often seen by our culture as a failure of the parents. We stand to lose not only our own esteem, but also that of the society at large. That's how I saw it. I felt that if Rachel killed herself, surely I had failed to fill some huge void in her that I had not even known about. At first I thought, "How can I live if she dies? How can I ever do anything again?" But then I began to feel it was a reflection on me. I felt ashamed when she even talked about suicide. It seemed like a complete repudiation of my life and values. Gradually as my daughter got help, and as I learned how to talk about suicide directly, the shame around the issue diminished. It had less power over me. Now when we deal with emotional issues, shame is not a dominant part of my response to her.

Religious Perfectionism

I was raised to be a good girl in a rigid, religious family. This religious perfectionism led me to think a person has to keep going no matter what. In short, good girls don't kill themselves. One might say my family of origin was religiously abusive: it praised perfectionism, excessive self-sacrifice, denying one's feelings, and living how others expected one to live. My family system never suggested that working hard had its downside or that sometimes you have to leave abusive situations in order to be healthy. There were no options. My mother's words were always, "Follow God's will. Your personal happiness is of no concern."

I have worked hard to counteract this grim message. But I had never before confronted one underlying aspect of my family's message: "Don't kill yourself because God will hate you." Though as an adult I didn't look on suicide as a sin, it was still, in my mind, something you're not supposed to do. I had often heard, "Your body is a temple. You use your talents to serve. Don't hide your light under a bushel."

Paradoxically, children present parents with the problems that are the most difficult for us to handle. I think they call it radar. In spite of all my previous work in therapy and Twelve Step groups, I was unprepared for the idea of suicide. As depressed as I may have been in the past, I never wanted to kill myself. I've always reacted to my problems by asking, "How can I change this?" or "How can I live with this?" or "Where's the door?"

If suicide was something many people did think about, then what was the next step? Spiritually, it was important for me to change my hateful and harsh internal belief to one that was loving: there was a loving God who wanted my daughter to live because she was loved and she deserved to have a good life. This is the message I presently believe.

Once I affirmed this new message by saying it over and over, I was able to let go of the old one and not be in a panic when talking about suicide.

Parental Love and the Preservation of the Family

After working through many intense feelings in the last five years, I've come to believe that human beings have a biological drive to live and that this is an instinctive part of life. Biologically, we need our children to continue and carry on our history. This feels like a healthy instinct to me. We have to go easy on ourselves when we first panic about suicide; part of our reaction is normal and healthy.

Aside from our fears of our own personal loss and our shame about being bad parents, there is also the elemental truth that we deeply love our children and we want them to live no matter what. Of all the people on earth, the one I would most readily die to protect is my daughter. I want her to live and live a happy full life. I honor this love for her as healthy, normal, and good.

First Things First

As parents, our personal feelings are important. But in the middle of a crisis, the first step is to get help for the child in danger. You may feel overwhelmed. Looking for help may take all your energy.

No matter. Stop doing everything else until you find help. If you don't know who to call for help, look in the front of the phone book for the number of a crisis hot line. Ask if there's a teen crisis line in your town.

If doing even this much feels too hard, you must call a friend to be with you. Ask a friend to help you make the phone calls. Ask a pastor or teacher for suggestions. Call the school and talk about the problem. Keep asking for help until you get it. Ask a friend to drive you and your child to the therapist or the hospital.

The next thing to do is to figure out how to deal with your feelings of fear and anger and shame so that you will be calm when you talk with your child. You have to be able to discuss suicide in a calm and thoughtful manner.

3

The Last Taboo:
Talking Directly about Death

> . . . pain is the root of knowledge . . .
> —SIMONE WEIL

Deal with the Reality of Suicide

In the beginning of the process of getting help for Rachel, one of the first and most important things I did was acknowledge her pain. I said to her, "I understand you to be saying you are in terrible pain. I will do anything to help you figure out what it is. I'm sorry I did not see you were in such pain sooner."

Secondly, I insisted she go to a counselor. She resisted, saying, "All my friends say therapists are full of shit." She continued to say that as she went to therapy. I said I knew it was difficult but the visits were nonnegotiable. You must get your child in to a therapist *fast.* Get the physical body there; don't worry about what you'll do next.

State the Obvious

You must tell your child that you love and want her or him to work through the pain.

As a teacher, I had been around kids long enough to know that it would not be helpful to say, "How could you think such a thing?" I also knew that I didn't want to tell her to shut up. Nor did I want to say, "Go ahead and make your own decisions." That seemed really cold. But I didn't know how to talk about "it."

Suicide is an act of violence, an act of self-destruction. It may seem horrifying to you, and you may have trouble expressing your love in the face of suicide. What helped me was to take out her baby pictures and look at all her natural positive energy and imagine that energy still being with her. I imagined her as a child swimming, playing by herself, counting pinecones in the backyard. I imagined all the active, energetic things she used to do as a way to keep in touch with the spirit in her that wanted to live. I knew that child in the photos was still inside her. But the part of her that felt joy intensely and passionately dealt with sorrow the same way. She needed guidance. So I set out to ask for help from friends who had been depressed and suicidal.

Talk about "It"

I sometimes wonder if the sexual revolution elimi-
nated sex as a taboo, and therefore the younger
generation had to find a new way to rebel, to be
shocking to the older generation. Could suicide be
the new taboo that must be toyed with? Or was it
something I'd never really known much about?

I started asking people in my peer group
whether they had ever wanted to commit suicide,
and many of them said, "Well, yes, I thought about
it." One day I spoke in a meeting of my Alcoholics
Anonymous group, and I talked about how upset
I was about the idea of suicide. In the past, whenever anyone in the group had mentioned
suicide, I had tuned them out—it was just not
acceptable. But that day I heard many stories from
people who'd once felt suicidal. I discovered it was
a part of many people's lives. I concluded that I had
been too repressed by religion to even consider
suicide. Perhaps thinking about suicide was a fair-
ly normal part of coming to terms with emotional
pain. When a person is in pain, working through it
includes the choice of feeling it or not, the decision
of living through it or not. In most cases, people
choose to live.

In the process of talking with people, a friend
who had been depressed and suicidal gave me a
book that has become my favorite: *Suicide: The*

Forever Decision. I highly recommend it, especially if it is difficult for you to talk directly about suicide with your child.

The author of this book, Paul G. Quinnett, talks directly to a person contemplating suicide. The first sentence is "The first thing I want to tell you about suicide is that you don't have to be crazy to think about it or, for that matter, even to try it. Suicide is a solution. . . ."[1] His matter-of-fact tone taught me how to talk about the subject. It helped me be conversational. Now I can say, "Suicide is a choice, but have you thought about the fact that your life may get better if you hang in for a while?" I became able to bring up the subject and converse in a normal tone of voice. When talking to Rachel I would say things like,

> Feelings change every day; you may feel great tomorrow. Life is about choices, and when you make the decision to die, you are saying that you don't have other choices. There are *always* choices. Have you really tried *everything* to solve your problems? What if you're depressed and there is help for depression? What if your thoughts change?

In the past five years, one of my most often-repeated sentences has been *There are always choices; you don't have to feel trapped; there are always choices.*

I also learned some things about botched suicides. This knowledge was useful to my daughter's recovery, to contemplate the fact that lots of self-destructive actions result in injury and maiming, not death. I said, "Do you really like the idea of spending your life in a wheelchair? You wouldn't be having much fun."

Take Only Long Enough to Make the Decision to Get Help

I've written more here than you need to know, probably, but since every family is different, I want to cover all the bases. The important thing is this: no matter what issues come up in your first conversation, *you must return to the nonnegotiable demand that your child get professional help.* The next step is deciding whether you have an emergency on your hands or whether you can wait to see a counselor within a week or so. Sometimes denial is so strong that parents don't see a problem until it is an emergency. If this is the case, go with it. Let it be an emergency. If you didn't see it coming, let yourself see it now. Don't be down on yourself because you didn't see it before—get on it now and *act.*

Part Two

Taking Action

Just for today I will try to
live through this day only,
not tackling my whole life's
problems at once. I can do
something at this moment
that would appall me if I felt
that I had to keep it up
for a lifetime.
—ANONYMOUS

4

Help Is There for the Asking

In adolescence, the Big 3 hits all at once—mortality, spirituality, sexuality.
—NANCY PADDOCK

Important points bear repeating: Suicidal children need to get professional help immediately. If you are the one who has discovered that your child is suicidal, you may need some guidance in finding a counselor. As I've mentioned earlier, if this is too scary to do alone—if you are a single parent or your spouse can't handle the stress—it's okay to ask a friend, a minister, or a relative to come and sit with you while you make the phone calls. Or you can ask them to help you make the calls. The first decision you will need to make is whether your child is well enough to stay home and see a counselor on an outpatient basis or whether your child needs to be at a treatment center or hospital in order to be protected from acting impulsively on suicidal thoughts.

"Is This an Emergency?"

When you call for help, you will probably be asked if it is an emergency. Is it? If your child has made a suicide attempt, you know it's an emergency and you've already called an ambulance. But what if there has been no suicide attempt? What if your child is talking about wanting to die, talking about wanting no more pain? You will simply have to talk with your child to determine how critical the situation is.

What do you ask your child? You say, "Can you make a contract with me that you won't do anything to hurt yourself for twenty-four hours?" If your child can't make this commitment, if your son or daughter says, "I want to die," then you have an emergency. You also have an emergency on your hands if you have discovered evidence of self-abusive behaviors, e.g., physical risk-taking, cutting, burning, or overdosing.

Another question to ask is "Do you have a suicide plan?" If your child says "Yes," you have an emergency. Nowadays, therapists focus on the plan as the strongest indication of danger. Sometimes people who talk about wanting to die can easily make a contract; they don't have a plan. The existence of a plan indicates that action is only a short step away. You must take this seriously and find a hospital or treatment center immediately.

Don't give up until you find someone to help you find a crisis unit, an adolescent treatment center, or a county hospital emergency room. If your child has a plan, put this book down now and take care of the crisis. Your child is your primary concern.

How to Find a Therapist

The school social worker who called me didn't think my daughter was in immediate danger. They thought she needed counseling, however. They would have helped me work through the system if I had not already had membership in an HMO. I decided to call the child psychologist there, knowing that if that person didn't work out, I'd look for someone else. As it turned out, that particular therapist, Carrie, helped my daughter cope initially. I'm using the term *cope* in a half-heartedly positive tone. Carrie helped Rachel deal with the issues around depression but didn't help her get through some of her feelings about major losses she'd suffered. Rachel talked to Carrie about her dad and her sadness over the divorce, but she didn't express her anger at him for not spending much time with her. Carrie's prognosis? "She probably won't deal with this until she's twenty-five." With hindsight I can see that this approach was a mistake. Rachel spent two more years in pain about her dad, not daring to tell him she was mad, not daring to tell me she was mad at me because she thought I was passive in dealing with him. When I find myself obsessing about what the first therapist didn't do, I tell myself that maybe Rachel wasn't ready to deal with her anger. Then I affirm out loud, "Every woman has her own timetable."

My daughter coped well enough to survive for two years, but then she went into a tailspin. She couldn't get off the couch, couldn't stop crying, and she talked about wanting to kill herself. She was having hallucinations about her own death. Although I didn't know it, she had a plan to kill herself. I knew we had to find some other kind of therapy. I felt desperate and grief-stricken. If Carrie had done everything she had thought possible and my daughter was still suffering, was there any hope?

When we, as humans, undergo therapy, we can only handle a few issues at a time. Rachel did as much work as she could with Carrie, and Carrie did the best she could at the time; yet the problem of suicide was not resolved.

How do you know if your child's therapist is a good one? My general answer to this question is simple: You know the therapist is good when your child is opening up to him or her, when there is some rapport. All of us find healing through our relationships with other people. This is true for work, for love, for church, for therapy. If there isn't open and honest communication going on, not much else can happen. If your son or daughter sits glumly, sullenly answering in monosyllables, then you know not much is happening in therapy. This process of opening up takes time, however. Don't rush it. I'd follow the recommendations given to people new to Twelve Step programs—suspend judgment for at least six meetings. Then ask if it is helping. If it is helping, your child will not continue to show the "signs and symptoms of suicide," as listed in the first chapter. If it is helping, your child will have work to do between sessions. Your child will say "Yes" to the question, "Does the therapist ask you questions that make you think?"

Even little changes can show a major shift toward recovery. Even though I knew wearing black clothing isn't a dangerous sign in and of itself, I was delighted when my daughter went shopping a year into therapy and picked out some spring clothes in yellow and lime and pink.

If you try one therapist and it's not helping after a few months, find somebody else. All the while, know that you may not be privileged to understand every facet of the process. You may not know for many years all the factors involved. So the best you can do is look for help and support, and take action in a crisis situation.

5

Dial 911: Taking Action

> As Dogen says, "A flower falls,
> even though we love it; and a
> weed grows, even though we do
> not love." Even though it is so,
> this is our life.
> —SHUNRYU SUZUKI, *ZEN MIND,
> BEGINNER'S MIND*

If it's an emergency, you need to act quickly. If your child has made a suicide attempt, call 911 for an ambulance immediately. If your child is talking about wanting to die and can't promise not to make an attempt at suicide, then find a crisis center. Nowadays most cities have a crisis line that can help you find an adolescent treatment center.

The day I took Rachel to the hospital was the holiday for Martin Luther King, Jr. I pictured him with his dream, his courage, and asked that she receive the same courage in her quest.

The point of this brief chapter is simple: You must put the book down and dial 911 if your child is in danger.

6

Inside the Heart of Despair: Asking for Support

> Oh, where can I go from your spirit,
> Or where can I fall from your face?
> If I climb the heavens you are there.
> If I lie in the grave, you are there.
> If I take the wings of the dawn
> And dwell at the sea's farthest end,
> Even there your hand would lead me,
> Your right hand would hold me fast.
> —PSALM *139:7–10*

This psalm is a comfort to me in three ways. It expresses my love for my daughter, it stands for my awareness of a higher power in my life, and it reminds me that my daughter also has a higher power. When I feel anxious about her well-being, I remind myself that no human power alone could have relieved me of my alcoholism; a miraculous higher power lifted me from my dependency. That same power is available to her.

When we live through a crisis, we may receive many miraculous gifts. We may experience our friendships in a new way. We may experience our spirituality at a deeper level. At every step of the way it is important to ask for support. It is important to think about what you need and keep asking until you receive it. Your needs will probably change in character as the crisis changes from an immediate to a long-term situation.

Ask for Help

When you ask people for help, proceed cautiously. Not everyone you know is going to be supportive of your situation. Some have an aversion to any situation involving hospitals, treatment centers, locked wards. Some are going to be judgmental about suicide. At this time you can't afford to be around people who don't support you. You need to take care of yourself, so don't feel obligated to discuss your situation with judgmental people. I've found that many parents with small children pull back when they hear stories about adolescents in pain. I feel as if I can hear them thinking, *"My* child, my darling sweetie, will never rebel like that!" When a child is in a severe crisis, parents don't need criticism or advice. We're probably already getting more than we know what to do with. So I simply thank them for their concern and turn to those who can really help me.

You *will* receive support if you ask for it. You will be surprised at the warmth and generosity you receive; there will be so much of it. It may come from unexpected people.

Personal support is vital to making it through this kind of stress. If you come from a background similar to mine, you may not have much support from your parents and extended family. That means you will have to work actively to find the support you need. You have to ask for help with practical things, like driving to the hospital, and for spiritual support.

During my crisis I felt really loved because of the people who came forward to help. I deeply value the friends and strangers who offered help. My sister and her husband were there every day. I've known people who don't have any living relatives; I'll always be grateful that my sister is here with me.

Another source of supportive people are other adults who care about your child. Think about who your child trusts and ask them for help: teachers, hairdressers, employers, and neighbors are a good start. I let Rachel decide who she wanted to come to the hospital to visit with her. The people she baby-sits for came to see her and brought their baby. It was wonderful to see all the other adolescents in the hospital flock to see the baby. The baby was so full of life, she gave everyone hope. I called Rachel's favorite cousin and asked him to call her. She was surprised she had a cousin who could connect with her pain.

Deal with Feelings of Hopelessness

You must find a place to turn when you feel hopeless. Some people in Twelve Step programs think of their friends as their higher power. Others have a strong relationship with God as they understand God, as a spiritual being. If ever I needed a higher power, it was when my daughter was in the hospital. I had a difficult time dealing with my despair, and I asked a lot of "Why me?" questions. Despair often washed over me with the same intensity it had before I sobered up. I felt powerless and inadequate. I felt like I had messed up my life. I also felt mad at God for giving me so many difficult problems.

My despair included feelings of hopelessness, shame, powerlessness, guilt, and anger. It included the hopelessness of thinking I would never break the negative patterns learned in my family of origin. I would come home from the hospital and lie down and think, "I can't recover fast enough. Why do I have to go through this too? Don't I ever get to escape the crisis mode of living?"

I didn't want to turn it all over to God. I felt like I would be surrendering Rachel's life, like Abraham putting his son on the altar. When I was a child, I didn't think Abraham should have put his son on the altar and, as an adult, I still don't think so. I don't have that much faith. Why would God want me to surrender my daughter? To write about it and then give others hope? No. I already did that about my family of origin and about incest. I don't want to keep undergoing terrible challenges just so the world can get the benefits of my experience through my writing. Let me experience some joy and I'll *gladly* write about that!

Finally I let my pain and despair be okay. There was so much of it, I would come home from the hospital and lie down and let myself just be in pain. At times I didn't want to talk with another human being. When I was really hurting, my chest felt like a flat, gray stone wall. All my sensations seemed to be focused on this emptiness. I felt carved out. I felt my chest was like the back side of the moon: gray, huge, pock-marked with craters, absolutely devoid of life.

At the same time, it had a shimmer like the new moon, where I could see the roundness. That was the odd thing: it was empty, I was empty, life was empty—but I didn't feel alone. I felt like the spirit of God was there with me, spirits of my grandmother, my brother, a presence, a resonance, a grounding voice that said, "I know it hurts." That's all—no promises, no cheerful hope—just a presence.

Acknowledgment. God does not like us to be in pain, but I believe God is with us when we are. I didn't feel the need to talk to another person in order to feel that I had been heard. I didn't feel isolated. I did talk to a lot of people for problem-solving. But I didn't *need* to do that to feel that I had been heard.

So in the end there it was, the surrender to God's will. If this is the way it was to be, I would accept it. I didn't like it, but I couldn't keep going on willpower alone.

Love Through the Pain

I didn't have much faith, faith in the sense that everything was working out for the best. I didn't have much hope. But I did love my daughter, and I had love for myself. A specific Bible verse hit me as though I were hearing it for the first time: "Faith, hope, and charity—and the greatest of these is charity." Love kept me going. My love gave Rachel hope.

By the time my daughter got out of treatment, I was determined to fight for the services necessary for her mental health with as much strength as I had, while at the same time surrendering her to the care of God. One friend told me what her therapist told her when her son slashed his wrists: "Some of our children get to grow and become giant oaks. Others are spring flowers. We love them and enjoy them whichever one they are." I don't think I've ever heard anything sadder than this quote. Yet it gave me hope. It gave me permission to keep loving my daughter as long as she was with me.

What can you do to gather a sense of love around you? Is there anyone you can call for support? When you hear the words *unconditional love,* which people come to mind? Have you met other parents whose children are suicidal? Have you talked with any of them and asked if you may call if you're feeling upset and offered your phone number too? Ask them for help now. To sit with you. To listen to you. To be available to you.

Then think of what you can do in your life to set up a network that will continue beyond this crisis. What do you need more of in your life? What would be the most relaxing and happy way to be with other people? Imagine yourself in a serene and beautiful place. Picture yourself at peace.

7

Courage: Giving Your Child Support

Courage is the price that life
exacts for granting peace.
—AMELIA EARHART

Anyone who agrees to go into a treatment program is showing great courage. Affirm your child's courage. Say things like, "I am so proud of you for having the courage to get better." Or, "I'm here for you." Consider what treat you could bring your child the next time you visit.

Each child may need different kinds of support. Rachel was happy when her aunt brought her family photos. Some children want to talk about what is happening. Other children become angry in treatment because it's the first time they've felt safe enough to express anger. So what will your role as a parent be?

Be open, be available, be ready to look at your own issues, and be ready to confront the treatment center staff if things don't seem to be going well. Adolescent treatment centers sometimes seem to blame the parents—you may feel that you are seen as *the problem*. Be ready to be open to your own failings *and* to stick up for yourself. You have the right to see the records, to have your concerns entered on the chart, to be consulted. Even though our children are *almost* adults, we are still the ones who are legally and ethically responsible for their well-being. It is frightening to turn them over to an institution.

Express Positive *and* Negative Feelings

The treatment center gave Rachel a break from her regular life. She loved occupational therapy. She met other kids who could identify with her depression. They helped each other with their self-esteem exercises. They traded information about ways to kill themselves and concluded that all methods were pretty gross, painful, ineffective, and difficult. There is no guaranteed way to die a painless death. There is no way to try to kill yourself with any certainty that you won't be physically disabled for life. Adolescents adopt a raw honesty when talking directly about suicide that can seem quite cold, but this coldness helped me get a grip on talking further about the subject. A year ago, I would never have been able to say, "I don't want to hear about you 'carving' on yourself with razors." Now I can say that in a conversational tone of voice. You may not think this is progress but in reality it was part of mine, and possibly yours.

Fight for Your Child's Rights

I had to stick up for Rachel's needs. That meant fighting with the treatment center about getting her into their day treatment program rather than going back to high school right away. I believed she was simply too fragile to go back to school. I had to fight for my rights as a parent, my rights to be consulted. Other parents I know have also had to fight both major and minor injustices. Examples include

- Mental health professionals who refer to parents in the third person as in, "What does Mom/Dad think about this?" while looking straight at us.
- Mental health professionals who start a meeting by reading the chart for twenty minutes, ignoring the clients in the room.
- Mental health professionals who call meetings without defining what the agenda is: is it a therapy session, a report to the parents, or a discussion of insurance coverage?
- Phone calls not returned.
- Mental health professionals who show ignorance and/or disdain for Twelve Step programs.

- Mental health professionals who do not confront fathers about their neglect and battering.
- The lack of legal means to force abusive parents to go into treatment.
- Mental health professionals who refuse to discuss the results of tests or make a diagnosis.
- Drug-happy psychiatrists.
- Mental health professionals who use the word *successful* when used in connection with a completed suicide.

It may help to take a few minutes now and do some writing about the frustrations you've been feeling. Then take a few more minutes to think about the people you could talk to about these frustrations. Writing down feelings is a problem-solving tool. It will help you see where your energy is going. It will help you find words to express yourself. It will help break big problems into small steps.

Honor your frustrations and anger. They can be a source of energy if they are channeled appropriately. My anger was an important part of the process of discovering the sources of Rachel's depression and in searching for the appropriate resource people and programs to help her. Anger jostled me out of guilt, fear, passivity, and the mistaken belief that some expert could "fix" the depression. I am grateful for my anger and its gifts.

Be sure to support your child's feelings of anger as well. When Rachel expressed her anger at the treatment center. I saw my role as twofold: I supported her in her anger, and I expected her to learn the things she could do to get better and then do them. I was fierce in telling her I wouldn't let her come home until she figured out a program for her mental health.

8

Drowning in the Romance Of Death: Fighting Back

> Only the good die young.
> —ANONYMOUS

Many parents worry about images of death in rock 'n' roll, never noticing that the romance of death is all around us. Part of the ability to deal with the idea of death and suicide is to demystify it for yourself.

Think back on your life and remember the stories you read that depicted death as a fulfillment, as a solution to pain. Think about the stories that depicted young people in a troubled situation turning to suicide as a solution. Doing so may help you see your child and family as part of a larger social pattern, and you will be able to talk about suicide with more ease.

The Romance of Star-Crossed Lovers

Did you read *Romeo and Juliet*? Even if you never read it, I bet you know the story. It is imprinted on our minds as a story of young love, a tragic mistake. But look at all the glory the lovers got. They live forever! Not only in high schools but in the play, the movie, and in the musical *West Side Story*. A recent research project surveyed the most commonly taught books in grades seven through twelve. *Romeo and Juliet* came in at number one with a resounding 90 percent.[1] This play glorifies suicide. I'm puzzled as to why it's the most often taught book/play. Do adults in our culture unconsciously glorify young love and the tragedy of an early death? Do we get hooked into the romance and fail to see how much we teach the idea that suicide is a solution?

There are also a number of movies that end with an early death presented as a solution. *Butch Cassidy and the Sundance Kid, Bonnie and Clyde,* and *Sophie's Choice* are just a few that come to mind.

Religion and the Romance of Death

In my personal deliberations on this subject, I also thought about the Judeo-Christian tradition, the primary images of Western civilization. The crucifixion is seen as a gift, a transcendence of pain. When Rachel went to Sunday school for a while, she wrote an interesting definition of who Jesus is: *He's a guy who let himself be hung for love.* She apparently didn't pick up the good news of the gospel message that since Jesus died, she didn't have to. You may scoff at her interpretation. But it is a *real* interpretation of what she heard. Perhaps she took in the image of the cross as her own personal solution. This kind of self-abusing interpretation of religion does have a history in Christianity, in self-flagellation, and whipping.

Maybe Rachel got the "wrong" idea, but the idea is there to be gotten. If you are not part of this tradition, take some time and reflect on the concept of death as it is presented in your religion. Is it a gift? Is it better than life? A reward? Whatever our religion, we must find ways to balance life and death. We must emphasize the aspects of religion that welcome living.

Other Images of Death

We can't talk about death and suicide without talking about the image of the mushroom cloud, the atom bomb that has been with us for many years. We live with images of missiles in silos, of toxic waste dumps, of a poisoned earth. At the same time we see pictures of wealth, glittering consumption, jewels, gold, and limousines.

Young adolescents take in these images and become overwhelmed by them if they have no way to express or release their feelings. And at times they reach out to the images of death in the world because these external images express their inner pain. When our children obsess about death images, we must find ways to give them life images through art, music, meditation, hugging, and tender loving care. We must insist that they do the work in therapy that will help resolve obsessive, violent thoughts.

9

Chemical Balance: Learning About Drugs

When I start going down, thinking about my life, I want to go out, smoke cigarettes and get high.
—DONNA R.

Any child who is depressed is at risk for chemical dependency. Any child who is depressed may be put on anti-depressants. You need to learn about both aspects of the pharmacology culture.

Drug Abuse: Self-Medication for Depression

Chemical use is often a factor in suicides. Many adolescents who kill themselves have been using or abusing chemicals to try to treat their depression. Unfortunately, drug use causes a descending spiral of depression. Initially, you need to find out if your child is using drugs. A chemical dependency assessment should be part of any mental health treatment program. You must stick up for your right to ensure this assessment is done. One mother insisted on a urine test to be sure her child was drug-free.

Many factors are at work within adolescents who are at risk. Your child may be primarily depressed but drinking to ease the pain, and therefore having a secondary problem with alcohol. It is crucial to detect whether or not your child is using chemicals, for chemical use is the cause of many adolescents' deaths. Many kids, like my brother, overdose accidentally and nobody can ever say if they really wanted to die. Sometimes kids get high and don't realize they're over the edge.

Anti-Depressants: A Useful Tool?

The last few years have seen a growth in the prescription of anti-depressant drugs as a form of treatment for depression and mental health disorders. There are many new anti-depressants and many people have learned by trial-and-error that they need anti-depressants to stay mentally stable. Many of the tricyclics have literally been lifesavers to suicidal people.

If a therapist recommends anti-depressants, ask questions about the particular drug, why it's being recommended, and what the side effects are. Discuss all of this with our child, who is the one who must deal with the side effects. It's important to say, "All drugs have side effects." (Anti-depressants shouldn't be given to people who are manic-depressive.)

Question Authority

Here is a little bit of our story for you to mull over. When the psychiatrist wanted to put Rachel on anti-depressants, he acted offended when I wanted to discuss the reason for it and the possible side effects. Her Minnesota Multiphasic Personality Inventory (MMPI) showed her depression to be average for adolescents. "We're not treating the MMPI," the psychiatrist said. The only reason he gave was that Rachel was not making progress fast enough and our insurance coverage was running out, so why not try the pills. That infuriated me. The second thing that infuriated me was that they told me I had to be in charge of dispensing the medicine. Here is a suicidal person who is supposed to be learning to be independent and take responsibility for her own life. And here is the mother controlling the drugs which presumably could cause an overdose if the child got hold of them. This would only create more tension and dependency between the parent and child. The third thing that upset me was that she did experience terrible side effects. What parent with a suicidal kid wants to find her unconscious? The psychiatrist acted like this was no problem. He acted as if her passing out and being "green around the gills" was no big deal. In the end, I believe she was less functional on the drugs than off.

Now, three years later, she has managed her depression and mood swings without anti-depressants. She continues to suffer from the pain of sudden mood swings, however, and is considering trying another anti-depressant. I support her in her search for stability.

10

Tough Love: Preparing For New Behaviors

> She looked so fragile,
> like a shell,
> the color of milk.
> —Brigitte Frase

A treatment program can provide a safe place for your child to begin to identify issues and feelings. It's a time-out. A place to rest and think things over. The time in treatment also gives you, as a parent, some time to work through your own issues and feelings. The goal of a crisis unit or short-term treatment program is generally to define the next step—a plan for healthy progress.

You will, however, probably have to start thinking about the next step before you think you are ready. You are going to be working through and feeling a lot of pain about your life. At the same time, you will be expected to make decisions about what's best for you and your family. The experts can help, but in the end the decision will rest on your shoulders.

Evaluating Your Child's Progress

How do you know someone is ready to come home? It's very difficult to tell. But the experts generally say that they don't want depressed adolescents to stay in the hospital too long because they can become so dependent on it that they won't ever want to leave. Here are some guidelines that can assist your family in getting ready.

Set Up a Long-Term Treatment Plan
You need to look at plans for continuing treatment after discharge. Such "treatment" could include a daytime program, weekly visits to a therapist, group therapy, adolescent self-help support groups, or a combination of these. It may also mean a group home, halfway house, or long-term residential treatment. The point is that you must think about the benefits of each choice and make a decision about what is most likely to be helpful to your teenager and to your whole family. The experts will make suggestions, but you don't need to be limited by them. Call people you respect and talk through the choices that are presented to you.

Write a Contract Together
Suicidal people of all ages are asked by their therapists and families to sign a written contract. This is a statement written in the person's own words

without any jargon or fancy talk. It simply states that the person agrees not to hurt herself or himself. It usually includes a list of at least three people who agree to take calls if thoughts of suicide become strong.

Therapists generally ask adolescents to list three responsible adults, not peers. The contract should be short and to the point. It shouldn't present a burdensome view of life. It is presented in order to give hope for leaving the safety of the hospital walls.

When my daughter was getting ready to come home after her stay in a crisis unit, I had two additional issues that I needed in the contract to feel safe. I said I preferred that she have no contact with her friend who was suicidal and refusing treatment; if she couldn't agree to that, I asked her to limit contact to three ten-minute phone calls per week. You may wonder how I arrived at any kind of decision about limiting contact. We all know that forbidding anything can really make a teenager hell-bent on breaking the rule. I talked with several of the therapists and the head nurse on the crisis unit and decided that limited contact might be okay because it wasn't "The Big No," but it also wasn't enough time for them to get into endless discussions of unresolvable problems, or as Rachel later put it, of nailing Jell-O to a tree.

After some initial resistance, my daughter agreed to this on a trial basis. It helped that I put the emphasis on the fact that experts say suicidal people shouldn't be around other suicidal people. I took the decision-making away from us and said, "Give yourself a chance to get better and follow their advice for a while." The other thing I asked her to put in the contract is still in force. No horror movies. Many of the images she was dreaming and hallucinating came from horror movies. I'm not saying the horror movies caused her suicidal fantasies, but they gave her visual images that expressed her emotional pain. When she saw certain images—people stabbing themselves, for example—all the emotional pain came back.

You may write this contract with your teenager and a therapist, or you may do it on your own without a therapist but make sure it gets done. If the treatment center overlooks this activity, don't let it slip by. Take care of it yourself.

Give Your Teenager Words of Hope
It is important for you to state your faith in your child's recovery. If you don't believe in it, who will? You are your child's best source of hope. Even if you are scared, express your hope in words you can honestly say. For example, "I know you want to have a good life, and I support you in your search."

"You can choose to work through your issues." "You can learn to control your thoughts." It is also important to say you will support your son or daughter returning to the hospital if need be. Write down the hospital's crisis number and say it is okay if they put it in their wallet and call from anywhere. It is going to be terrifying to leave the security of the hospital.

You might ask the responsible adults on the contract to look for positive changes and give your child feedback now and then for the "good stuff" they see happening.

Learn about Things to Do When
Images of Suicide Appear
This kind of talking is different from the contract talk. The contract is a commitment. A "Things to Do" list involves a wide range of choices, depending on the day. When depressive or self-destructive images appear, it is important to learn how to change the movie being played in our minds. We can choose to change what we are thinking about. Some activities help us change the movie: exercise, listening to peaceful music, going out and renting a comedy. The following list, adapted from *The Courage to Heal,* can get you started talking with your teenager about a list of options.[1]

Things to Do When I'm Desperate . . .

- Breathe.
- Put on a relaxation tape.
- Call Natalie.
- Call Vicki if Natalie's not home. Keep calling down my list of support people. (Put their names and numbers here.)
- Eat Kraft macaroni and cheese. (Not an option for a person with an eating disorder.)
- Start again at the top.

When my daughter and I talked about this list, she laughed at the idea of macaroni and cheese. She loves it, although I usually encourage her to eat something more wholesome. So she loved the idea of a list that gave her permission to indulge in a favorite food.

The treatment center may also give your teenager a list of things to do when he or she starts to get down. It may include suggestions like "Keep a list of people you can call by the phone," or "Don't stuff feelings."

Even though you put energy into establishing these guidelines, you can expect to have much anxiety and fear on the day your son or daughter comes home. It is helpful to act as if you have hope even when you are filled with fear. It is helpful to remember to breathe, to find the place in yourself that believes in this person's recovery. Say affirmations for your child's recovery. Here is one mother's affirmation: *Infinite intelligence within Michelle will always lead her to do the right thing.*

11

Honest Eyes: Making A Commitment to Family Therapy

> If our kids have lived with
> parents who have been in pain,
> then our children are probably
> in pain too.
> —MELODY BEATTIE

When our children are in such pain that they want to die, we must acknowledge that something has to change in their lives. Something in our family life has to change. But what? There are so many possibilities. The thought of suicide fills us with fear and terror, and it's difficult to look at the situation objectively. The possibilities of what we could be doing wrong are endless. We may feel defensive and say, "I'm about average—how come my kid is in so much pain and my friends' kids are soaring?" We may be so overwhelmed with shame and guilt and despair that we can't do anything to change.

We may also retreat into denial and announce that it's all the fault of society, rock music, or our ex-spouse. We may be willing to send the child to therapy but refuse to take part ourselves.

During the last few years I've had all these feelings. I've gone through fear and blaming and feeling average and dumping on myself. I've gone through the regrets, thinking things would be different "If only I had realized sooner that I was an alcoholic." I felt my life was falling to pieces. I had that desperate feeling that so much had gone wrong that I couldn't ever have a happy life, and that I had hurt my daughter beyond repair. Then I simply started working on the issues at hand.

Doing Whatever It Takes

If we want our children to get better, we have to be willing to go to family therapy. We need to be willing to go without knowing what's wrong. Once in therapy, we can ask the fearful questions: What's wrong? What has to change?

We will eventually discover something we can do to make the family situation healthier. Just as we only live one day at a time, we work on one issue at a time. Out of the huge fog of fear and terror and confusion, we will discover answers. I am not the perfect therapy candidate; I've often been defensive. But I've learned to say, "Yes, I'm feeling defensive about what you're saying. Give me a minute and I'll let it sink in."

My daughter has ultimate responsibility for her own life. In therapy, she learned some skills for building her self-esteem, for dealing with depression and mood swings. She also worked on issues about expressing anger to both her parents. She talked to the therapist about her feelings for her dad, the divorce, and about being adopted.

In family therapy, I learned I had to change some of my attitudes and behaviors. The most immediate things the therapist asked me to work on were

- Don't fix, don't explain.
- Make a truce with Rachel's dad, my ex-husband.
- Listen to her anger and pain about her stepfather.
- Spend more time talking and state my feelings more often.
- Stop using humor as a defense during serious discussions.

Some of these items seem to contradict each other. For example, *don't explain* may seem like a contradiction to *spend more time talking*. Much of recovery is paradoxical. I needed to stop explaining in a codependent way and talk more in a conversational way.

I could not have made these changes by myself. Nor could I have made them with the help of family and friends, mainly because my immediate circle sees me as a good listener—a good mother. And I was. But I didn't know how to listen to Rachel's pain.

Therapy is a forum, a ritual way of talking, which gives more importance to words than a typical conversation in the kitchen receives. Much of what Rachel and I said in therapy—acknowledging our pain and anger and hurt—we had said to each other before. But we didn't know how to listen to one another. I had avoided sitting and hearing her pain. I didn't want to take it in. And my main defense was humor—to sweeten up the scene and move on. The result was that she hadn't felt *heard*. Therapy provided a forum for us to communicate directly. It was a ritual, missing in the rest of the culture, that could and did allow us to be closer to each other.

Addiction: A Family Disease

All of these problems that got addressed in family therapy were related to issues in my childhood, the abuse in my marriages, and my drinking. Like many alcoholics, I was a functional drunk. My daughter doesn't remember ever seeing me drunk. The reason she doesn't remember is because I was a quiet drunk for the most part and quit drinking when she was eight. I was quiet and happy when I was drinking and denying the havoc around me.

I had thought I was making progress in my second marriage because Jim, my second husband, never beat me up like Rachel's dad did. But he too was filled with rage. He would go on a verbal rampage about once a month and anybody who got in his path was his target. When I faced the pain his rage had caused Rachel, it didn't give me much comfort to know I had made progress. Even though I learned how to draw the line on his emotional abuse, my daughter was deeply hurt by his rage. I continue to make amends to her by the way we live now and by my commitment to be in healthy relationships. When Rachel told the therapist about Jim's verbal abuse, her description was so violent and painful the therapist believed she had been physically abused. Rachel related the following story to her:

> I was sitting on the top step above the landing going upstairs and he came up and stood on the landing staring at me. I don't like people to stare at me. His face was red and all the veins in his forehead were popping out. He said, "If you don't stop crying, I'm going to pound you into the floor. If you think I'm going to stick around here and listen to this, you're wrong." And I felt like I couldn't breathe, like he had something around my neck and was going to hang me.

Recovery: A Family Process

Hearing my daughter in such pain taught me several things. It taught me again how much words can hurt and that she needs to be heard when she has been hurt. It reminded me of the verbal abuse of my own childhood and how much I had repressed it. It taught me to be gentle when I talk to Rachel. The positive result of having all this pain in the open is that we are both so aware of how verbal abuse can hurt. We have made a commitment to each other not to be in abusive relationships. We talk about our relationships with other people—friends, peers, and my family of origin. We are learning how to say, "that hurts" when someone says something verbally abusive. We work on this commitment together.

These were the issues that the therapist led us to—and through. Other issues also created changes in our family life. I have set up a more routine schedule now than I had before, with grocery shopping and other chores on specific days. I talk more *directly* with Rachel about our schedule, rules, routines, and feelings. These changes made an enormous difference in the sense of stability in the family.

What Are Your Family Issues?
What Needs to Change?

What I've related about our family issues may not be your family's concerns at all. I simply wanted to talk about some of the specific issues I dealt with first as a point of connection. I hope it will help as you look at your life.

In my reading and discussions with other parents and experts in the field, I have concluded that nobody has the slightest idea about a profile of a typical "suicidal family." In fact, I now believe that suicidal thinking may be even more common than I thought and that there are probably many profiles of a typical family, and all of them are accurate.

Following are some of the ideas and issues I've learned about that you may need to face in therapy. By "face in therapy" I mean that painful choices may lie ahead. There are no two ways around it. In order for the family to change, each person has to make some changes. As our therapist says, Rachel's happy with her home life now because she feels she's got me in her life for the first time.

Family Issues and Suicidal Adolescents

Many of the experts on teenagers and suicide seem genuinely baffled. In fact, no one has been able to predict which kids are truly at risk for suicide. But there are some life-and-death situations that do have a devastating effect on children. When these events occur, we need to give children more attention and guidance than ever before. For example, if a parent commits suicide, the children certainly will be haunted for the rest of their lives with thoughts of following this example. All children of suicides need to find special attention and support. Families with histories of depression and suicide need special help. Children who live in a family that is experiencing extreme problems, such as unemployment, chronic illness, and depression of one or both parents are certainly at risk. We might even say that these families fall into a category called Depressive Families.

There are other family situations that are generally regarded as very destructive situations for children to live in. These situations are often cited as factors for children at risk. As you read along, consider which of these situations could be a true factor for your child. Look at your family realistically.

You may not be able to identify problem areas by yourself. You can go to a therapist and simply say, "I don't know what I'm doing wrong. I'm willing to look at my life."

I heard one therapist say, "In families where there is a suicidal child, in some way the family is not being open." Outsiders thought that our family looked loving and open, but in some ways it wasn't.

I didn't comprehend how Rachel's losses had affected her.

One expert, who wished to remain anonymous, says suicidal kids are *usually* from families where the mother is overinvolved and the father is emotionally absent. Unfortunately, that includes about 90 percent of the people we all know! This comment makes me mad because it is not helpful; it's a guilt trip. Yet look at what this might mean for you, even if the idea is as common as watching the ten o'clock news. Work through your defensiveness. What would have to happen in your family for the father to be more involved?

From these general descriptions, you may not have much of a sense of what you can change. A therapist can help you explore the possibilities. The process of therapy helps us change concepts into behaviors.

Abuse and Its Relation to Suicide

There may also be dangerous things happening to your child that you don't know about. You need to learn what is and isn't dangerous.

Studies show that many suicidal teenagers have been abused. You must determine if your child is being abused. The most common forms of abuse associated with suicidal teenagers are listed at the top of the next page.

- Sexual abuse.
- Alcoholism, chemical dependency of family members.
- Physical abuse.

Sexual Abuse Kills the Will to Live

Many children who attempt suicide have been sexually abused. This is true for boys as well as girls. Most have been abused by an adult in the family or a trusted family friend in a position of power over the child. When you are wondering why your child wants to die, one of the first questions to ask yourself is if your child has been sexually assaulted by someone you know. Why is this one of the first questions? Sexual abuse is devastating. There is a straight line from it to self-destructive behaviors. If it's hidden and secret, its power may block any work on other issues until it's out in the open.

Some children are too ashamed and scared to tell until years later, but these same children might have opened up earlier if a therapist had gently yet directly asked them, "Has someone touched you in a place you didn't like? Did someone make you take off your clothes when you said stop?" Direct questions may end the silence.

The Price of Active Addiction

As many as four out of five adolescents who attempt suicide may be adult children of alcoholics.[1] What is the connection between alcoholism and suicide? It may be that drinking while pregnant gives the baby a predisposition to depression. Children learn despair through body language. When a parent is drinking, the person is simply not available to the children. Yearning for death comes out of this emptiness. The parent who is drinking or engaging in other addictions is not available to deal with the feelings of the children. Usually that parent is also not dependable, not keeping a routine, and not providing the predictability children need to feel secure.

Of course, there are other family situations that can cause a parent to avoid feelings and behave in unpredictable ways. Often the behaviors of a depressed person are very much like those of a practicing alcoholic. Children are set adrift when they don't have their feelings affirmed and a routine in place. The point is that many situations may cause this kind of neglect, but you need to consider whether alcoholism is present because it is destructive to children—and it is very common.

Alcoholism is so common that it is possible that the 80 percent figure I quoted earlier is actually higher, when you consider that AA is anonymous, and that often mental health professionals don't discuss addiction right away. Nobody at Rachel's treatment center asked her about a family history of addictions. From what I've seen in other families I've met through treatment and Al-Anon, there is also a connection between adult children of alcoholics families and suicidal kids—I call it the second generation legacy of the despair of drinking. The inability to show feelings gets passed on, even when the drinking doesn't.

What is your family's history with alcohol? Is there alcoholism in the generation that came before you? If so, there may be dysfunctional methods for dealing with feelings that have probably been passed down.

And what about other compulsive behaviors? Is any family member abusing drugs, gambling, overeating, using sex in a compulsive manner, or compulsively shopping? Anyone who is showing these behaviors needs to be working a recovery program. No one can have a good relationship with an addict because an addict by definition is unable to have good relationships with people.

If you are drinking to excess and denying that your drinking is a problem, you need to deal with it honestly before you can expect your child to be happy. You cannot maintain an addictive behavior and have the energy to take care of your child's needs. If your spouse or partner is an addict, then you are also playing with fire. The consequences are life-threatening. If you are living with an addict, you are giving too much energy to that person because he or she is taking energy from you with or without your consent and you simply won't have the energy to give the attention your child needs.

When I first started going to Al-Anon, I thought it was a magic program. It isn't. I learned I couldn't live with an addict and be a good parent. Some people have been able to use Al-Anon and stay in their marriage, but I wasn't able to do that. I was so preoccupied with my husband's unhappiness and trying to control his rages that I had little energy for anything else. I had to leave him to have the energy to be an effective mother. Rachel needed more of my love and attention.

If there are no problems in your immediate family, you might want to look at your family history. You must confront the legacy of addiction and dysfunction in your family. I grew up in a family that offered us a shame-based religion, the silent treatment, physical violence, and sexual abuse— all in a house of teetotalers. This greatly affected my ability to express feelings and develop healthy relationships. If you are an adult child of an alcoholic, what issues are you working on?

Openness to your children's feelings is the key here, as is openness to having a good parent-child relationship. If you don't know what this phrase means, you need to find a therapist who can help you figure it out, either by yourself or with your children.

Physical Abuse: Seen and Unseen Wounds

Children who are hit and children who witness other people getting hit develop many symptoms.[2] They are at risk for chemical abuse, school problems, and stress-related ailments. Experts say these "negative relationships" in the home lead to suicide.[3] What is the history of physical abuse in your immediate family and in your family of origin? What is the connection between physical abuse and rage? Is there an adult in your family whose anger is unpredictable? Are your children getting hit or living in a home where they witness other people being physically abused? Your child will probably not get better while living in a violent situation.

Rachel's father was a batterer. My daughter doesn't remember seeing him beat me up, but she did witness it. Sometimes I would be holding her when he started beating me. She's picked up my fear and anxiety. Like me, she jumps, startled, at the slightest noise. Even at the age of sixteen, she cries when it storms and thunders. Leaving that abusive situation was critical to Rachel's and my mental heath.

Dealing with Labels

If you felt depressed, anxious, tense, angry, or sad when you read the previous section, stop and imagine for a minute all the other people who live in similar situations. Trust me, you are not alone. It is estimated that 80–95 percent of all families could be labeled dysfunctional.[4]

If I had seen myself in all the negative labels that are bandied about in self-help books, I'd never get out of bed in the morning. If I internalized everything that has been said about battered wives, alcoholics, codependents, adult children of alcoholics, and incest survivors, I would have a laundry list a mile long of my deficiencies and the desirable qualities I lacked. All the labels may be true, but there is more to me than labels.

When I first heard that many incest survivors become chemically dependent, I felt ashamed because that's what I did. Then, after some more work on the issues, this fact became a relief. I said, "I'm glad my life is a cliché—it means that I have a lot in common with a lot of other people." I decided not to cave in to the negativity in my life, and to take credit for my work toward recovery.

Those of us in recovery have a new vision of family life that is free of shame. We have a vision of ourselves as healthy, responsible, and joyful people. We have become life-affirming, rather than the walking wounded.

The medieval mystic Meister Eckhart said, "Whatever God does, the first outburst is always compassion."[5] Have compassion for yourself, for where you've been, for your struggle. Let go of the past and its death and pain. Have mercy on yourself.

12

Hope: Breaking The Negative Cycle

> . . . visiting the iniquity of the
> fathers upon the children unto
> the third and fourth generation.
> —*NUMBERS 14:18*

The idea of despair and pain repeating themselves generation after generation is the most painful idea I know. I want to break the cycle of abuse and depression and pain. When I see the hurtful patterns of my childhood repeating themselves in my life and my daughter's life, I really have to struggle against despair.

When we are in despair, we are of no use to our children. Underneath my despair is often shame and the fear that I've damaged my child, that we will never recover, that the cycle will go on and on.

That's when we most need to find hope. When I recognize I'm falling into despair and shame, I deal directly with the labels my mind throws up in my face—those words that come out of psychologists' reports and studies, such as *overinvolved mothers* and *Adult Children who . . .* These words can cause me to feel sad and ashamed and discouraged. I can say, "What's the point of even trying?" Once I was at a conference and a psychologist said, "Incest victims are the most difficult to treat." I felt ashamed, even though the speaker didn't intend to be shaming. Other descriptions have had the same effect on me. When I first went to Al-Anon and read the handout called *Characteristics of Adult Children of Alcoholics,*[1] I thought, "Wow, this is really a heavy load to overcome."

Now I have a more gentle attitude toward myself. I may decide this is my year to work on self-acceptance. Next year I'll work on money problems. I don't have to do everything at once. So if my child is in the hospital, this must be the year to work on my issues dealing with motherhood. It's time to turn my attention to her and our relationship.

Dealing with Shame and Despair

None of us has been the perfect mother or father. There is no such parent. When we make a mistake, we need to break through our denial, admit that what we are doing is hurtful, and then work on changing our behavior. We can ask God to remove our imperfections—in my case, my anxiety, my fear, and my desire to crack jokes rather than cry. God does not want us to wallow in pain over old mistakes. We are supposed to get on with our lives. How can this be accomplished? I remind myself often, "We are all creatures of the earth. We have feet of clay. We are not birds of the air. We are not the dolphins of the sea. We are not the forces of nature: fire, lightning, wind. We are simply creatures living a physical life who make mistakes, who learn slowly, who sometimes even might be called slow learners."

When I work on changing my behaviors and releasing despair, I use affirmations and private rituals as a form of prayer, conducting some traditional spiritual practices. My spirituality is a hodgepodge of beliefs and practices, and the organized groups I belong to offer a lot of room for personal interpretations and practices.

Which practices from your heritage could help you deal with your shame and despair? Which new practices could be of use to you?

Jill Breckenridge, author of *How to Be Lucky*, has written affirmations in response to the list of Adult Children of Alcoholics, often called the "Laundry List" of adult children of alcoholics. Affirmations are positive statements that can be spoken out loud or written. They help bring a new reality into being when they are expressed. When I am in despair, I focus on one affirmation and write it down over and over. Then I say it as I take my walk. The Laundry List, written by Tony A., and Breckenridge's affirmations (in italics) appear below.

Characteristics of Adult Children of Alcoholics and Affirmations to Heal These Dysfunctions

1. We became isolated and afraid of people and authority figures.

   I am connected to others and hold my own.

2. We became approval seekers and lost our identity in the process.

   I am God-centered and seek approval from God for who I am.

3. We are frightened by angry people and any personal criticism.

   I accept criticism serenely as a chance to grow.

4. We either become alcoholics, marry them, or both, or find another compulsive personality such as a workaholic to fulfill our sick abandonment needs.

   I no longer fear abandonment.

5. We live life from the viewpoint of victims and are attracted by that weakness in our love and friendship relationships.

   I give up being a victim and help others overcome their victimhood.

6. We have an overdeveloped sense of responsibility and it is easier for us to be concerned with others rather than ourselves; this enables us not to look too closely at our own faults, etc.

   I take excellent care of myself and do a constant self-inventory.

7. We get guilt feelings when we stand up for ourselves instead of giving in to others.

   I stand up for myself willingly.

8. We became addicted to excitement.

   I am committed to a level, serene life.

9. We confuse love and pity and tend to "love" people we can "pity" and "rescue."

   I choose equals who can return my love and support.

10. We have "stuffed" our feelings from our traumatic childhoods and have lost the ability to feel or express our feelings because it hurts so much (Denial).

    I feel and express my feelings and needs easily. I breathe deeply, and my feelings flow through me.

11. We judge ourselves harshly and have a very low sense of self-esteem.

    I am gentle with myself and give up perfectionism.

12. We are dependent personalities who are terrified of abandonment and will do anything to hold on

to a relationship in order *not* to experience painful abandonment feelings which we received from living with sick people who were never there emotionally for us.

I ask only for God's will for me and the strength to carry it out.

13. Alcoholism is a family disease and we became para-alcoholics and took on the characteristics of that disease even though we did not pick up the drink.

    I work the Twelve Step program.

14. Para-alcoholics are reactors rather than actors.

    I actively love myself and my life.

Private Ceremonies, Visible Prayers

Once I wrote a short poem about Rachel and her identification with coyotes. When she was seven, she had a T-shirt with a coyote howling at the moon. She wore this to bed every night and it kept her safe. At the same age, she would make a ring of her stuffed animals around her bed to guard her— gray kitty, lion, snakes, bears, and coyote. In the poem I talked about her reluctance to grow up. When she became suicidal I was filled with terror that I had somehow romanticized her childhood and was holding her there. Had I given her the message not to grow up? I was filled with remorse and regretted ever writing the poem or calling her "Coyote." Then one day when I was shopping, I found a beautiful pair of coyote earrings. I bought them and wore them every day, saying as I put them on in the morning that the spirit of the coyote would call Rachel back to life and be with her into her adulthood. Somehow this was one of the most inspiring prayers I've ever had. It's given me the power to hope.

Traditional Spiritual Practices from Your Heritage

If you are connected to a spiritual tradition or religion, this is a good time to ask yourself which practices could be useful to help you hold on to hope. Is there a community ceremony that focuses on hope? Is there an elder, a spiritual leader, or friend who can pray with you? Is there a ritual for cleansing and healing?

Every religion—Western, African, Asian, American Indian—has ceremonies for forgiveness and healing. Twelve Step programs have a structure for renewal, the Fourth and Fifth Steps. At one point in my work I did this formal process concerning my life as a mother. The effect of the process was very powerful.

Other Sources for Spiritual Renewal

Let yourself relax and think about the informal and unstructured activities that give you the deepest sense of wholeness. Maybe you can take some time to go out of doors and rediscover your sense of serenity. The sky and the earth restore our sense of self-worth and hope. Or take an hour to lie on the floor, listen to your favorite musician, and let yourself think hopeful thoughts. Take the time to visit a friend who restores your sanity, connection, and spirit.

13

It's a Jungle Out There: Looking at Other Issues

> The order that the mind
> imagines is like a net, or like a
> ladder, built to attain something.
> But afterward you must throw
> the ladder away, because you
> discover that even as it was
> useful, it was meaningless.
> —UMBERTO ECO

Every way of looking at the world has its limits. As imperfect humans, we don't have one single world-view that can explain everything or guide us always.

I had to be open to see things outside my world-view. As you know from the last few chapters, I see the world through the eyes of a believer in Twelve Step programs and family therapy. But I realize that a single outlook does not work for everybody. In fact, whenever we accept one view, we often tend to shut out other information that may be useful.

Experts on adolescence have said that to be healthy, teenagers need to have a sense of belonging in three areas: home, school, and spirituality. We've delved deeply into family matters, so let's take a closer look at school and spirituality.

First, take a few minutes and forget everything you know about family systems and addiction and look at your child separate from the family. Besides family issues, what has been bothering your child? What are your child's continuing obsessions? Animal rights? Pollution? A feeling of not fitting in? Worry about being good enough to get into college? Think about what you've head your child say, and try to remember if any sentences have been dominant, such as "I'm so dumb." Take stock of what is happening in your child's life.

School

Many adolescents feel pressured by school, by expectations about college, and by the pressures to conform that have always run rampant in American high schools. There's acute tension in almost every high school in this country to fit in, get high, dress the right way, wear your hair right, etc. As our therapist remarked, "It's a jungle out there." It's probably worse now than when we were in high school because the culture has become so much more materialistic, sexualized, and greedy.

Appearances are more important than ever before. So you might consider what kind of pressures your child has at school. Ask your child that question and listen to the range of answers. Does it feel like there are secrets, harassment, or tensions your child can't verbalize? Is your child saying something that doesn't fit into the pattern? Is your child being harassed for being different?

Rachel had gone around saying, "I'm so dumb" for several years. I knew she was smart and perceptive, so I couldn't understand where she got this idea. When she was in treatment and would say she was dumb, the staff and her peers would say, "Uh oh, low self-esteem. Gotta work on that."

Six months after treatment, Rachel got very angry about school. I didn't know what it was about and neither did she. One October night in 1989 we watched *The Cosby Show.* On this particular episode, Theo was diagnosed by his college teacher as being dyslexic. At every turn of the plot when Theo described a problem with learning, Rachel would say, "That's how I feel, Mom." For example, Theo said he studied hard for a test but when he read how the question was worded, he went blank. Rachel said, "I do too." The show was a revelation. I was amazed. Another piece of the puzzle fell into place. I called the school social worker the next day, and they tested her for learning disabilities. She has major problems with dyslexia, a term the professional educators don't use. Her disabilities affect her reading, paraphrasing, memory, and the ability to understand abstractions and process information. It's difficult for her to get the letters on the page to "hold still" long enough to get the ideas into her brain. I discovered she can read out loud faster with the book turned upside down than she can "the right way." She had done a phenomenal job of getting by at school by overcompensating, listening, even cheating on tests. Oddly enough, her disability makes it easy to read her neighbor's paper during a test! Her teacher and school counselors praised her and affirmed her in her struggle. The school social worker said, "It's amazing what you have accomplished."

I felt guilty that I hadn't figured it out earlier, relieved that we had another piece of the puzzle, and angry at the school for not recognizing her problem. All my anger passed as Rachel made her way through two special education classes and got tutoring for her academic classes.

After a year in special education, she was still struggling with school. Her anger was reduced, but school was still a struggle. A psychologist and her teacher recommended that she be evaluated for attention-deficit hyperactivity disorder (ADHD), an evaluation that can only be done by an M.D. The disorder results in distractibility—a short attention span. Every sound in the room has equal value—the gum wrapper, the ticking of the clock, the teacher's voice—so that paying attention to the flow of the class is difficult. The evaluation process for this disorder moved quickly, probably because it made sense. The minute Rachel heard the checklist of symptoms, she laughed and said it sure sounded like her. Besides distractibility, the disorder causes symptoms like impulsivity and problems with aggression.

There's a lot of misunderstanding about ADHD. It's a malfunctioning of the brain that affects not only school performance, but also relationships with people. It may or may not always include physical hyperactivity. Many girls who sit and daydream in grade school, like Rachel, are not diagnosed because they are not causing trouble. Boys, on the other hand, can get a reputation as a behavior problem, rather than a diagnosis and help. This is an example of how covert sexism harms both boys and girls.

We're just beginning to understand how this disorder has affected Rachel's whole life. It seems to have connections to her hot temper and her frustration at communicating. The impulsivity seems to be connected to her accident-prone personality, her early sexuality, as well as suicidal thinking. This is the young woman who had an accident the day before commencement but walked to the stage on crutches as if she didn't have a care in the world.

In the meantime, Rachel reflects on her life with a philosophical bent much wiser than her years. She has great wisdom about life that coexists with her impulsive nature. There was a joke going around that posed the question, "Have you heard about the dyslexic atheist? She didn't believe in dog." When Rachel heard this joke, she turned quite philosophical. She said, "You know, Mom, I remember the day I realized that *dog* and *God* were the same word. I was jumping on the bed at Kathy's, so it had to be first grade. I thought to myself as I was jumping, if it's the same word, when you spell *doG,* do you capitalize the *G?*" These were serious questions to her that she never asked. No wonder this child had so much trouble in school. It breaks my heart she didn't get help earlier. As she says, she thought everybody saw things the way she did, so what was the point of asking.

Spirituality

Most teenagers feel better when they feel they belong to something larger than themselves—a group, a spiritual community. But even if you raised your children in an established religion, they may not have received the idea that they are loved by God. Some messages from church come through as shaming and perfectionistic.

If you have not been involved in an established religion, what can you do that helps your child develop a spiritual sense, a sense of being at one with and loved by the universe? My daughter resisted joining a church. We visited several kinds of religious communities. What she likes is for me to read her meditations from a book by Diane Mariechild, *Inner Dance: A Guide to Spiritual and Psychological Unfolding.* These meditations create physical relaxation, a sense of peace, and visions of universal connection between people and all living creatures. I see this and her love for music as Rachel's source of spirituality. She has acquired a fondness for environmental sounds, New Age music, George Winston, and electronic music, which she listens to at night when she goes to sleep.

For several years she wanted me to read her meditations, and fortunately, her mind internalized the form. When she spent the summer with her father, she had a bad motorcycle accident. She told me, "I lit my black candle, watched it, then I closed my eyes and made up a meditation about the ocean waves washing all the pain and stiffness out of my body." I think she is learning to take care of herself without me.

In addition to school and spirituality, I also suggest that you look at the issues in parts 3 and 4 and ask yourself if any of these issues are affecting your child. For example, is it possible your child is struggling with sexual preference? Many suicidal adolescents are struggling with this issue, terrified to talk to their parents for fear of rejection.

Be open to listening to issues that might be bothering your child that do not get categorized in this or any other book. This is what people mean when they say, "Listen." Listen, keep listening. Sit on the couch, pretend to be half-asleep and listen. Give your child a ride, turn off your music, and listen.

14

It Takes Life to Love Life: Self-Care for Parents

> If allowed, time and nature will heal you. Remember that you do not have to heal yourself. Nature is ready to do it if you step out of her way and do not present her with those unnecessary obstacles, despair and disappointment.
> —Dr. Claire Weekes

As you continue working through the process of family recovery, it's easy to get discouraged. It's easy to get into the habit of negative expectations and wonder, "Now what's going to go wrong?" It can seem so overwhelming.

As parents, it's important for us to work our way out of negativity. We can't blame ourselves for not figuring out everything our child needed. We're human, and we can't always have everything figured out. This is one of my biggest lessons from the last four years. It is still hard for me to accept that I don't get to be perfect. It hurts to know I'm human! Perfectionism is one of the legacies of my childhood—I believed that my job is to always solve the problems. With it comes the related belief that I'm not supposed to *have* any problems, and that the sign of a really together person is someone without problems. We're always going to have problems, and they have nothing to do with our personal worth.

When I start asking myself why I didn't do better or why I couldn't see this coming, I stop and think of the ocean, washing up green, glass baubles, dead fish, beautiful driftwood. I think about how life washes up on us without us really knowing what's coming next. We don't know what life will bring. We can't see into its depths and know what the next wave will hold. All we can do is deal with what comes to shore, the beauty and the pain. Even if our child dies, we have to go on. We have to choose to give up negativity and despair and find beauty in our lives.

Getting discouraged is a signal that you need to take a break. What could you do that would bring you pleasure? What can you do every day to stay centered? Can you take some time now to take a walk and get some fresh air? Are you eating good food? What are you doing today to foster the belief that you, as well as your child, are a beloved child of the universe?

Take some time to do something that will help you find serenity and fun, even in the midst of the chaos. Let go of trying to control the outcome of your child's life. Do what you can and then take care of yourself.

The paradox of letting go of controlling your child's life is that you may suddenly see that child even more clearly than you did before. It is wonderful to find a positive memory of your child and hold it as a symbol of the life spirit. Can you think of one moment of your child's life that you will always hold precious, regardless of the path your child takes? Here is a touching example of what I mean, written by Cary Waterman.

Climbing Mount Washington

There is an old photograph on my desk of my son Devin taken just after he and I reached the top of Mt. Washington in the White Mountains of New Hampshire.

We had all started out together that day—my mountain-climbing brother, Chris; his wife, Cindy; my daughter, Amy; and Tony, my companion of many years. Chris and Cindy were familiar with the terrain. In fact, I had hiked here many times when I was younger. But the years had taken a toll and as we started out it was clear that Devin and I were going to be the slowest. I had the excuse of having smoked for many years. I don't know what Devin's excuse was. It was 1982. I was 40. He was only 13.

I remember that he had on some loose-fitting tennis shoes with broken laces and no socks—clearly not the thing for hiking. So we were in general unprepared and on Mt. Washington that's not a good idea; at 10,000 feet the weather can change quickly and the temperature had been known to plummet 30 degrees in minutes.

As the trail narrowed and got steeper, Devin and I fell behind. Soon we lost sight of everyone else. And then, coming to a fork on the trail, I directed us off onto the wrong path. We hiked another three miles before we saw a sign and I realized we were going the wrong way. By now we were both hot and sweaty and not having much fun. But Devin had his heart set on getting to the top. We began to retrace our steps. I remember the trees were close by the side of the trail and we both were thirsty. My brother, of course, had the only canteen. I didn't know at that point if we could get back on the right trail and still make it to the top. We had lost a lot of time.

As we went on, Devin got more and more upset with the way things were turning out. His feet kept flopping around in his shoes and his face was streaked with dirt. Finally, he sat down in the middle of the trail and started to cry. "Now we'll never get to the top," he sobbed. I told him we would still try to do it just to get him up and moving. We finally got back on the right trail and set off up the mountain. My plan was to go part of the way and see what happened. I'd say to him, "Let's go a little further and see what happens." We started and stopped, started and stopped. Other hikers passed us. Like the tortoise, we just kept going. I thought we'd see our family but we never did. Soon we were above treeline. The granite mountainside fell away from us into a deep gorge. The trail became steeper and we scrambled over continuous boulders. I was breathless, but the scenery was so beautiful.

It was colder up here but fortunately we had jackets with us. We didn't have any gloves though, like most of the people who passed us. And we were going so slowly. One of us would stop and the other one would go on a ways and then wait. If one of us got too far behind, the other would yell back, half nagging and half encouraging. It was like leapfrog. But when we got within sight of the summit, Devin took off with what must have been a thirteen-year-old burst of boy energy and disappeared. I sat down; I didn't think I could go any further. And then he was back, with my brother in tow who had been all over the mountain looking for us. The rest of the group had only gone half way up before they went back down to find us. Here we were—the only ones besides my brother to get to the top! I struggled up the remaining 100 yards or so, my legs snapping like rubber bands.

In the years since then, when it hasn't been easy going between Devin and me, I've remembered us climbing Mt. Washington many times.

I've had a hard time letting him go to make all the mistakes I guess he needs to make.

He's had a hard time becoming responsible. I've been frustrated and angry with him and I've felt despair about his future. I've worried about him and I've been scared for him as he tried to move away from me. Sometimes it's been really hard to believe he would be okay. Often it's been hard to trust.

So finally, I got out this photograph of him at the top of Mt. Washington. He's got one foot propped up on a rock like the conquering climber, his hands in his pockets, and his jaw set pretty toughly against the cold wind. Behind him I can see the White Mountains and a few clouds and the blue sky.

—CARY WATERMAN

Part Three

Dealing With Adolescent Issues

When an adult acts foolishly, when we want to pass judgment, we say he or she is "adolescent." Today's adolescents are adrift in a society that gives them neither the actual time and attention or a sense of tradition to try to sustain them. This is as true for adolescents in suburbia as it is for those living on the streets. The latter may be more damaged and in greater pain, but all adolescents live in a world that fails to embrace them.

—BRAULIO MONTALVO

15

The Family Community: Coming of Age

> Can we offer our adolescents
> something of substance,
> ends as well as means to
> nourish their development?
> —ROBERT TAIBBI

Adolescents in our culture are in a tough situation. There is no rite of passage to mark the change from childhood to adulthood, so our kids kind of mush around in a twilight zone for a couple of years, gradually assuming adult responsibilities with no clear affirmation from society that they're going to make it into the world of adults, or even that they've been accepted. Other cultures around the world do observe rites of passage that help the adolescent move from the magical time of childhood to the world of responsibilities. The rite of passage is a marker, a boundary, a transforming experience, respected by adults as legitimate. You may know about many of these ceremonies, such as the vision quest among some American Indians.

In our present culture, what experiences are similar to a rite of passage? Are there rituals that mark the passage to adulthood? Voting? Driving a car? Drinking? For those who are religious there may be a ceremony such as confirmation or bar mitzvah/bas mitzvah, but these ceremonies are not acknowledged by the larger community. For some young men, coming of age may be marked by joining the armed services. Often it seems that young women announce their adulthood by getting married or getting pregnant or both. But while these gender-based behaviors may serve the purpose, they don't affirm the whole person in a nurturing way. It's become the responsibility of the family unit to deal with the enormous changes on a family-by-family basis—each family creating its own community and ceremonies.

What holidays does your family celebrate? What new family traditions would you like to have with your family? Who do you see as being part of your community? What could you do to start a new family tradition? To inspire you, listen to one adolescent's wish:

> It's okay, I guess. I go home and watch my soaps and MTV, and talk on the phone, but I really wish my mom and I had more time. I guess you could say I miss her.[1]

As parents we need to build a community for our children to be part of with us. We need to structure ways to spend time together and affirm their passage and worth as community members. We have too often believed the myth that adolescents want only to be with peers. Yes, peers are important, but when young people are asked directly about what they want, many say, "I want to do things with my family—go to movies, play card games, talk." We need to continue family activities even during times of crisis.

16

Changes: Adolescent Loss And Grief

> Loss is another word for change.
> —M. TATING

One of the primary tasks of all adolescents is say-ing good-bye to childhood. This task has elements of pain, as well as nostalgia and bittersweet senti-mentality. For adolescents who are facing other losses such as the divorce of their parents, the normal task of saying farewell to childhood may be doubly overwhelming. When we think about the fact that almost half of our children have parents who have been divorced, we realize there is much grief work to be done.

Children need to say many good-byes: to lost pets, to grade school friends, to the timeless days of summer backyard play, to bedtime stories, and eventually to the daily nurturing love of parents. A person of any age who does not say good-bye to a real loss will continue to carry that loss. Losses accumulate in our psyche. They're like tin cans hanging around our necks, clanking and dragging along, interfering with our present reality until we face and release them.

There are steps we can take as parents and helpers to ease this process. We can identify losses with our children, we can let our feelings about our own losses come out, and we can learn new techniques for bringing some resolution to the grief. Most importantly, we can learn to listen when our children express pain over a loss. Experiencing the pain of loss is the first step in letting it go. It is a violation of the human spirit not to let someone experience a loss. In other words, when a loss occurs in our child's life, we listen to the pain and don't try to fix it. If a pet dies we should not gloss over the pain and get a replacement fast. We need to let the pain be there.

Identifying Losses

One way to begin to identify where we've been and what we've lost along the way is simply to make a list of losses. When we sit down and write out a list, we think about big losses and little losses from our whole life. We remember how it felt to be eight years old and lose a blue jacket at the park. We remember what it was like to be in seventh grade and lose self-respect when other kids teased us about the funny clothes our parents made us wear. We remember how it felt the first time somebody we loved moved away. We write down losses that other people might find trivial. We ignore the tapes in our head that say, "That was such a long time ago." and "That happens to everyone." and "That was such a little thing, how can you still remember that?" and simply catalog the losses we remember.

My daughter and I have talked about losses, especially during therapy sessions when we were dealing with loss. I've made a list of my losses, and talked with her about some of my feelings.

My list of losses:

- Loss of childhood and trust due to sexual abuse by my dad.
- Loss of brother through death.
- Loss of secure job, dropping out of graduate school to put my husband through medical school, loss of academic life.
- Losses that came about from drinking and codependency, trying to please my husband (the stagnant years).
- Problems with self-esteem.
- Loss of cherry desk, marble table, and other furniture.
- Little Bear, the cat who thought she was a dog.
- Bride doll's wedding dress.
- Quit my job to follow husband's career, denying the hurt.

- Miscarriages: no more babies to hold.
- Even at age forty-five, wish that I had nurturing parents.
- I still miss my grandmother, who died in 1984 at age ninety-eight—why couldn't she still be here?
- Purple dress.
- Missing having a lover but not willing to have one yet.
- Blue bathrobe.

As I look over my list, I see that I started out with the big losses that I know from therapy and moved on to more "feelingful" writing as I went. When we write lists, we can be free to change the language as we go; I started off by starting each line with the word *loss* and ended up with some comments written straight out as I thought them. If you write out a list of losses, let the words come out any way they want to.

Rachel's list of losses:
- Pets: two hermit crabs, cats (Rocky, Little Bear, and others).
- Floppy the bunny, all my goldfish, my two favorite African water frogs, my snail, all the homeless kitties that my mother throws out of the house.
- Friends: losing them from moving around, losing touch.

- Boyfriends.
- Biological parents because I was adopted.
- Turquoise elephant that played "You Are My Sunshine."
- Books I loaned to friends.
- Rings and earrings.
- Dad moving out of state.
- Losing big house when Mom got divorced.
- Being a little kid and playing with no worries or sense of time.
- Special papers with stories, I don't have them.

When I hear her list, I no longer want to rush in and fix it. But what do we as parents do about the sorrow? First, we listen. We listen to our own hurt and to our children's. We say, "That is really sad. I wish you hadn't lost that." Then we say, "What else do you feel besides sad?" Relief? Longing? Anguish? Irritation and aggravation? Compulsion to replace? Fear of abandonment, fear that if one parent left you, another one might? Anger? I've found that a short conversation can be very revealing. One way you might begin is simply to share your own list with your child. You might talk about some of your feelings around your losses. If it's not possible or appropriate to talk about your list with your children, it's okay to drop the conversation and move on to something else. There are other ways to express the pain of loss besides talking.

Expressing Sadness over Loss

After we make a list of losses, one of the best ways for getting at the feelings of sadness is suggested by the children's book *The Tenth Good Thing about Barney,* by Judith Viorst. In this short picture book, a family talks about their dead pet by thinking up ten good things about their pet. I've used this idea in my own grief work in my journal. I've also used the idea when I talk with my daughter. When we moved out of our house I said, "Let's talk about all the things we liked about this house." The birch tree we planted, the roses, and the big room where I could lie in my bed and look out the window and watch the streetlight are three that came to mind. Words bring the sad feelings to the surface because the loss is attached to the very concrete pictures we get from "the good things."

In the initial stages of expressing loss, we should never underestimate the intensity of our children's sadness. When I work in schools teaching children how to write, one of the most striking elements of their writing is its intensity— and one of the most common comments from teachers and other adults is "It's hard to believe that a child could express feelings that intensely." It seems to me that in this culture we have a myth that children are basically happy-go-lucky, they are resilient and can survive anything. This has some truth to it but the intensity of grief is the flip side of the resilient child. For example, in the following poem we can feel the intensity of the loss. We can also see that the child is still experiencing the loss and afraid it will continue to be with her forever.

Fear

He walked out of my life at two
and came in and walked out at three.
Seven was when he came here and I
saw him last.
He walked out that time too.
I have the fear of never seeing him again.
At thirteen he sent a plane ticket so I could fly out.
One month I spent with him and all the time having
the fear of leaving.
I have the fear of him leaving my life for good.
I have the fear of him.

—RACHEL FIRCHOW

Writing about feelings is something that both grown-ups and teenagers can do. It is useful to find ways to express loss, especially when we are stuck at a distance from our feelings and not able to cry. As parents, we can work with "pieces of grief" with our children and let the therapists go after what we don't know how to handle. Therapists can also help us understand losses we didn't know were there.

I've noticed in our family therapy work that often working with anger will unlock the feelings of loss. If we can't connect to our own pain, maybe we can connect to anger about betrayal, change, loss, divorce, and death. It is said that anger is often a cover for a deeper feeling like hurt, shame, or fear of abandonment. When we express anger, we often cry and go deeper emotionally to feel the hurt for the first time.

Other Feelings Connected to Loss

When we think of loss, we usually think that the feeling we must get over is sadness. While sadness is the most immediate feeling identified with loss, there are other feelings and intensities of feeling as well. Think about the difference between losing a devoted grandfather through death and leaving a favorite book on a school bus. You might be mad at yourself for forgetting the book, but the book is replaceable, your grandfather isn't. Not only might you be upset that you didn't fully express your love to Grandpa, but you'd feel anguish at the thought of never seeing him again. I don't want to minimize the effect of losing a favorite book, but we have different kinds of feelings about different losses.

I've experienced other feelings that come with loss and grief too. Shame is what I consider my primary negative feeling, and it surfaces with every stressful situation, which includes all losses. In the event of any loss, I have to work through the shame of it, as well as the other feelings.

With Rachel, I see that a present loss triggers her earlier losses, bringing to the fore a fear of abandonment that she experiences as a paralyzing force. One day when we were talking about this in therapy, she said to the therapist, "Every time my mom walks out the door, I think she's never coming back." I reassured her that I will not abandon her. I'm here for her. And we're in therapy to help her escape the grip this fear has on her.

In order to fully feel loss, I also have to accept contradictory feelings. For example, when we sold our house, I had many feelings raging within me: shame, relief, hurt, jubilation. When we are experiencing such a dichotomy it helps to ask, "What am I ambivalent about in this situation?" If I can accept the conflicting emotions, I will be more receptive to feeling them. I've noticed that has given Rachel relief to say, "It's okay to have more than one feeling about things."

As Dr. Richard Obershaw, a Minnesota therapist, has said, "Grief is the process whereby an individual reidentifies who they are, following a loss/change experience."[1] He suggests asking ourselves three questions to help resolve our feelings: "What have I lost? What do I feel about the loss? Who am I now?" The framework of these questions provides a most thorough way of working through some issues that may arise.

Who Am I Now?

After a loss our job is to reestablish an identity. Another way to express this is to say we need to bring resolution. We need to see ourselves as whole people without the beloved person (object, situation, or fix) in our life.

The following suggestions are some ways of reestablishing an identity after a loss.

1. After you have identified your feelings about a loss, try writing new descriptive names for yourself, like these: "I am a young woman, a child of divorced parents, who is learning how to be healthy." "I am a young man who has survived his negative feelings." When you give yourself a new name, you give yourself credit for the work you have done.
2. Write a good-bye list.
3. Write out a list of opposites: I used to be _____, but now I am _____. For example, "I used to be a twenty-two-year-old in graduate school, dropping out to take care of my husband. Now I'm the author of three books. Another example, "I used to keep my anger bottled up. Now I know how to yell and call a friend when anger overwhelms me."
4. Collect pictures that symbolize the loss. (Photos or drawings.) Throw them in the trash. Cut them up and say good-bye. Throw your

good-bye letter in the river. A ritual usually adds additional power to your words.

5. Pray to let go of wanting to hold on to the lost person or experience.

6. Write out a description of what you wanted to have happen. When you are done, write *but this was not to be.*

7. Write affirmations that affirm your right to grow and change. *I am a child of the universe, loved and beloved. I belong here. My life is unfolding according to a divine plan. My life is manageable and guided by my higher power. My feelings will not kill me.*

Many of these activities can also be done by adolescents. You know your child better than I do, so you know which activities might be useful. You might start with making your own "Loss List" and trying one of these other activities a few weeks from now. My daughter loves to make pictures and collages. One way we have worked through loss is with pictures, through a picture collage of people we love: those we've lost and those who are now in our lives. Adolescents usually love to work with colorful pictures. Perhaps the pictures express new, intense feelings that they have not yet found the words for. Suggest that your child draw favorite scenes from childhood. Or draw pictures of places in the present that are sources of peace.

If you want to rush right out and replace what has been lost, take some time and think about the idea of replacements—some things can be replaced, others can't. We can't always will or demand a replacement. Often we receive a friend when we are least expecting one.

When Rachel and I were talking about all the lost things we missed, she remembered losing her favorite stuffed animal when she was three. After all these years, she still missed it! It was a turquoise elephant that played "You Are My Sunshine." She lost it in a house we were considering renting. When we got home after looking at the house, she realized her elephant was missing. We drove straight back to the house and looked in every room, but couldn't find it anywhere. The people who owned the house hadn't seen it either. The mystery was never solved. A few days after telling me about her memory, she walked into a music box store and discovered a green dragon that played the same song. It wasn't soft and fuzzy, but it was a close enough match. After thirteen years, and after many other soft animals, she finally felt content with her loss. Maybe it was also expressing her feelings that brought the resolution. Maybe she was ready, after thirteen years, to listen to the song again.

There are many books available that deal with loss. You might want to do some work about your own life separate from your issues about your children. One useful book, *The Grief Recovery Handbook,* has a plan you can work through with a "grief partner," a friend who also wants to work through a loss.[2]

Many other books have thoughtful ideas. You might investigate support groups for grief issues. Whatever method you choose, the key is to get going, because your unresolved losses will continue to affect your life and the life of the family. The ambience of sadness is overwhelming to children's psyches. Unresolved grief is deadly.

17

Tied Up in Knots: Stress

> The degree of stress is not as
> important as an adolescent's
> belief that he or she possesses
> strategies to deal with the stress.
> The fear of not being able to
> handle losses or disappointments,
> even in successful adolescents,
> concerns them greatly.
> —WILLIAM PORTER

Many adolescents who look like they're doing well say they feel continually stressed and pressured. Some experts have noted that any time there is a "population bulge" there is an increased suicide rate in the young. Our present generation of young people is one of these bulges. Consequently, there is stress on the social services in the schools and other organizations that serve youth. Kim Smith of the Menninger Clinic says, "There are still only so many slots on the football team. . . . The message implicitly given by society's institutions is more likely experienced as, 'There may be too many of you; you are expendable,' rather than, 'Welcome, we need you.'"

From this, it would appear that *all* adolescents of our children's generation need to be talking about their stress levels and working on ways to feel their uniqueness and value. What exactly does a stressed person need to do? A healthy lifestyle with good food, relaxation, exercise, and regular communication might sum it up. How many adolescents do you know who are able to practice such a healthy lifestyle? How many of us adults truly practice a healthy lifestyle? It's something to aim for together.

When we look at our children's lifestyle, we need to be aware of school stresses and the other factors that are affecting them. Then we need to make stress-awareness part of our vocabulary. We need to have healthy expectations within the structure of the family. But the kids are the ones who have to take responsibility for their own health, in this area more than any other, perhaps. When they leave the house, they choose whether or not to get crazy on Camel straights, caffeine-laden soda, and junk food.

Do You Need a Stress Test?

A few years ago a life-changes stress test was popular among adults. I was curious when I found this test adapted for children in the book *The Hurried Child: Growing Up Too Fast Too Soon,* by David Elkind.[1] I was curious to read the test, but I was not in a hurry to let my daughter take it.

When I read it, however, I was appalled to discover that some experiences I had deliberately brought into her life because I thought they would be valuable turned out to be stressors. For example, Elkind lists as a stressor the following: Starts a new (or changes) an extracurricular activity. This activity change is something I encouraged Rachel to do every year! I didn't think it was good to make kids take piano lessons for ten years. Why not let them pick one new activity every year and explore the world? So Rachel has taken lessons in piano, guitar, karate, and swimming. It's hard for me to think this was a bad idea. Yet here it is in black and white. And it was rated at thirty-six points!

"Parents divorce" is ranked at seventy-three points! Oddly enough there is no stress factor listed for family violence. I thought it was better to get divorced than raise her in a family where she would have to see her mother beaten up every few months. In fact, the test presumes "normal" families with no hitting, no drugs, no abuse. So I see I've not only caused my daughter stress by getting divorced, but also by whimsically letting her choose a new activity every year.

Sarcasm aside, I've concluded that I don't have to be mad at David Elkind for insinuating I'm a bad parent. I am both in charge of my life and power-less over it—I made my decisions in good faith.

When we checked the book out of the library, the librarian said, "I took that stress test for adults and the results said I was due for a nervous break-down but nothing happened. Don't take it!" But Rachel wanted to take the test. The book says, "If you child's score is above 300, there's a strong like-lihood he or she will experience a serious change in health and/or behavior." Rachel's score was 563—higher than crisis. We knew that before she took the test.

Stress Relievers

Rachel's focus in treatment has been on her depression and anger, and stress seemed to be a secondary issue that would take care of itself when she learned how to deal with the other issues. After she got out of the hospital, she was interested in handling her stress level. She talked about it a lot. She had a great class in health. I think she's the first person I ever met who liked her health class! The teacher liked her, and that seemed essential to her learning. The class did a unit on healthy lifestyles, and each student did a self-assessment of their lifestyle. Rachel's score put her in the "Hazardous" range. I wondered what in the world she was doing to rate as hazardous. It turned out she was putting herself in jeopardy by her crazy sleeping habits and her reliance on sugar to get through the day. I didn't know at the time that she was drinking three huge bottles of soda a day with a high sugar content. After this assessment she made some changes in her eating habits, especially her sugar intake. She became more consciously responsible for her diet, health, and exercise. Exercise is essential for the release of anger, guilt, shame, depression, fear, and stress. How wonderful that she figured out what to do.

Be Patient with the Mystery of the Process

One day Rachel received a letter from one of her friends from treatment. She said she had gone back into the hospital. Her letter said that the day before she went in, she didn't have that much to eat, and she and her friends sat around all day smoking, drinking coffee, and talking about suicide. Her physical stress level contributed to her uneasy emotional state. It's surprising how such prevalent and simple substances such as sugar, nicotine, and caffeine can speed our bodies up to the point that we're feeling stressed and anxious.

Adolescents must learn to monitor the behaviors that contribute to their stress level. This is one area where parents really need to let go; it really is out of our control. If our children are stressed, we can provide some guidance if they can't figure out where the stress is coming from, and then be open to talking about choices for the situation.

It's important for you and your child to talk openly about stress. It's important for your child to have a commitment to certain activities that reduce stress and to be accountable for maintaining these activities. Maintaining a healthy lifestyle is especially important for suicidal kids—they react quickly and desperately when their stress level is over the edge.

18

Fiery Zits and Sudden Outbursts: Anger

> Anger is a great energizer if you
> don't get stuck in it.
> —LaVonne Stewart

Adolescents often have a lot of anger and don't know where to put it or how to express it. Like all of us, they need to learn to express anger directly in a nondestructive fashion. Many adolescents who have been raised in a family with problems are quite understandably afraid of anger—afraid both to feel it and express it. Others are acting out angrily because they have experienced so much anger around them. Anger is the jack-of-all-trades for many adults, the expression for all buried feelings of hurt, shame, and fear.

It's not always easy to tell how your child is feeling. Rachel always looked happy-go-lucky until she crashed. Then she expressed negative feelings toward herself. Part of her early work was to learn how to move from self-destructiveness to anger.

Rachel's therapist, Barbara, had her make an anger jar. She told Rachel to take an empty peanut butter jar and fill it up with slips of paper, each one with the name of a person she was mad at. These people could be from any time in her life, and they could represent little and enormous angers. It takes lots of little pieces of paper to fill a peanut butter jar, but Rachel kept at it and pretty soon it was full. In fact, it was so full the pieces of paper stuck out the top and flopped over like a house plant. At the next therapy session, Barbara asked Rachel to pull out some of the slips at random and talk about her anger. This exercise gave Rachel permission to see her anger in a tangible way. It was okay to be mad.

Other suggestions for dealing with anger:
- Closing the door to your room and yelling.
- Beating a pillow with a tennis racket.
- Running hard for a long time.
- Calling a friend.
- Speaking with "I" statements, "I'm really mad."

The therapy process helps people take the next step, which is to deal directly and assertively with the situations making you mad. Barbara taught Rachel how to do this.

Becoming Empowered to Take Action

The word *empowerment* suggests that as we feel more powerful within our own world, we will be able to channel our anger in positive ways. People who see their actions having an effect on the world have a strong sense that anger can sometimes create change for the better. So we need to look for ways to empower our children. I have noticed that adolescents' anger decreases when they find a way to channel some of it into working for something worthwhile. During adolescence the great surge in hormones is accompanied by a growing awareness of all the injustices in the world. Why not find a channel for this energy? Rachel has become interested in animal rights. I hope she becomes more involved on a political level because she has the energy for it.

You might do some thinking about available activities that could give your child a chance to grow, develop potential strengths, and become empowered. Often having the responsibility for a task that no one else is going to do will give kids a sense of empowerment. Find out if someone needs to have a pet looked after. Is there someone in your neighborhood who needs help one morning a week? Rachel helps a blind woman who lives in our apartment building. She also has "big-sister" responsibility for two young children she baby-sits. These two little kids say there's nobody like Rachel. Nobody could take her place.

Programs like Outward Bound and other special camps offer challenges to young people that give them great self-esteem. They also provide a release of pent-up negative feelings. The young people become empowered by becoming stronger and discovering they can do more than they thought they could.

Consider as many of the choices as possible for your child.

19

Depression: The Heavy Cloud

> There is either a "vacuum"
> where feeling should be, or there
> may be a feeling of heavy,
> pressing depression (the "horse's
> hoof") on chest or abdomen. . . .
> —DR. CLAIRE WEEKES

Many of us are depressed at some time in our lives, but when adolescents become depressed, many also become suicidal. It is important for them to work their way out of depression because it is a life-threatening condition.

Feelings Associated with Depression

Sometimes depression takes a person by surprise. The person is suddenly incapacitated without knowing how or why. William Styron has written a book, *Darkness Visible: A Memoir of Madness,* about his experience with depression that can help us as outsiders understand this condition. He says that the illness is like a physical pain that becomes so unbearable that death seems to be the only way out. "It doesn't have the exquisiteness of a broken limb but it does have a suffocating quality, the feeling of being trapped in an overheated room."[1]

Some say depression is anger turned inward. This may not be the whole story, but any discussion of depression has to include anger and shame and guilt. One of Rachel's primary tasks was learning to move from depression to anger. The next step was from anger to assertiveness.

Sometimes anger may be a reaction to feeling overwhelmed, an inability to see choices. And life is all about choices. When we're depressed we feel helpless. The first thing we need to do is make one choice, do one thing, ask for help. This is true for us at any age.

Learn to Express Many Feelings

Many adolescents end up being depressed because they feel unable to articulate their feelings of anger, sorrow over loss, shame, longings, hopes, and dreams. Depression becomes the world of no-feeling. Many kinds of classes, workshops, and therapies can help them learn to express their feelings more directly. Rachel said she didn't feel she understood the relationship of anger to her depression when she got out of treatment, even though it had been discussed. On her own, she looked for a class and signed up for it. It was called "Shame, Guilt, and Anger: An Introduction for Women." It was a beginning class in identifying feelings and learning some assertiveness skills. It wasn't therapy, it was a *class,* with slow explanations and handouts and role-playing. Rachel seemed more able to learn from this class than from group therapy. Looking back, it seems to me that her learning disabilities have interfered with her ability to process information in discussion group settings. She does better one-to-one with a therapist or with a basic class. If your child is having trouble understanding all the relationships between these feelings, consider whether the information can be given in a more understandable way. Research all the resources in your community to find those that best meet your child's needs.

Create a Structured Life

Learning about feelings is one of the necessary steps in dealing with depression. It's equally important for the child to make a commitment to self-care: a structure, a routine, a list of acceptable behaviors. Certain behaviors are *mandatory,* as Barbara, Rachel's therapist, said, "So you don't go down so fast."

Adolescents have to learn their own warning signs; nobody can do it for them. It's important to do the routine things that keep us sane:

- Exercise
- Good food
- Contact with a friend we can be honest with
- Appropriate therapy/learning about feelings
- Adequate sleep

Helpful Hints along the Way

Many of the remedies for dealing with depression are also the remedies for anger and stress. Creating a structured life, having a program of self-care, and regularly exercising are crucial for mental health no matter how our negative symptoms are expressed. I've come to believe that for adolescents, many different symptoms are different aspects of the same pain. I see these negative feelings as a big knot. When we loosen and let one feeling out, the other feelings are loosened up and need to be expressed and released.

The pain of adolescence is connected to a growing awareness of the human condition, the consciousness of injustice, and the expression of the losses experienced in life. It is also the expression of the fear of growing up, and anxiety about change. As adults, we must continue to talk to them, affirm them, and listen to them.

On the other side of pain is the discovery of self-worth. As our children work through their depression and deal with difficult, sometimes negative, feelings, we need to give them credit for the good qualities they have. One item on Rachel's list is "Notice what you do well and praise yourself." This is very difficult for any depressed person to do, but a friend can help. Giving praise to each other can become part of family communication.

20

Just to See You Smile: Caretaking

> I spent my childhood walking on
> eggshells, trying to keep the
> peace in the house. I would do
> anything to keep my dad
> from getting mad. It took all
> my energy.
> —MICHAEL L.

C *aretaking* is a term that means spending more energy on other people than you spend on yourself. My working definition today is that one would sooner take care of someone else's need than his or her own.

Children as Caretakers

Caretaking is encouraged by our culture. Caretakers want everyone to be okay, and they'll do almost anything to see that that happens. Caretakers have somehow decided that the way to be valued in this world is to do good things for others. Now it may be a good idea to do good things for others at times; the idea becomes a problem when caretakers neglect doing good things for themselves. People who spend their lives focused on others end up being resentful, angry, exhausted, out of control, and depressed.

Many suicidal kids have been busy looking out for their parents' welfare. Their own feelings get out of control because they're putting all their energy into making life okay for everyone around them.

One boy in treatment told of becoming enraged when he was biking with his mom and she didn't look both ways at an intersection. He screamed at her, cursed her, cried, and could not continue on their bike trip. He was so heavily involved with her well-being that he couldn't enjoy their time together. The parents had recently divorced, and the boy was reacting to the loss and change by taking too much emotional responsibility on himself. In treatment he learned he didn't have to protect his mother; it wasn't his job to make everyone else in the world happy.

I would bet that every depressed adolescent has been heavily into caretaking due to some imbalance in the family system. When a child is caretaking, there's an element of over-responsibility for a parent. The result of this caretaking for the child is a depletion of energy, the suppression of natural joyful feelings, and then depression. Caretaking becomes a bad habit. Caretaking robs us of vital energy—it robs us of our life force. In fact, we can see our work through and out of depression as a journey to discover the real person who is hiding there, lying on the couch watching reruns. Working through anger, loss, shame, and fear releases a person to discover the real self, the real strength and character.

Rachel as Caretaker

It saddened me to discover that Rachel thought she had to protect me from her father. She was caretaking both of us. She put out lots of energy trying to make peace between us. She covered up for him so I wouldn't get upset. I couldn't always see what was hurtful to her. Some things she didn't want to tell me out of loyalty to me. She had information she thought would hurt me if I knew it. It did hurt me when I heard about it in the therapy session, but I was willing to hear it. For example, her father had often talked about me in a disparaging way when she was at his house. He said things like, "There's no problem in this world that takes four years of therapy. Look at your mom, she's still got problems after all this therapy." This put Rachel in turmoil because she wanted him to be nice to me. She was suffering the loss of her parents as cooperating partners and exerting too much energy trying to make us get along with each other. Not only did it take her energy and put her in turmoil, it made her scared to go to therapy herself for fear he would ridicule her.

Once Barbara discovered the extent of Rachel's covering up, she helped Rachel let go of it. "Your mom can take care of herself," she said. I learned how to let Rachel know she didn't have to protect me.

Give Up the Habit of Caretaking

No matter what age they are, in order to work through caretaking, kids need to start looking at who they really are—what they feel, what they think, what they want, what they like, what they need, and what they're good at doing. They need to figure out how to believe that it's okay for them to give some of their energy to themselves. They need to believe that they, as much as anyone, deserve to have a good life. They don't have to help other people to feel good about themselves. They don't have to protect everyone else in the world.

There are many ways to let go of caretaking. There are books that can help you and your adolescent in this process. *Codependent No More* by Melody Beattie is a good place to start. If your child is not a good reader, you can get this book on tape.

You and your child could go to Al-Anon and Alateen. Or take a class in assertiveness training, for the flip side of caretaking is assertiveness and self-worth.

As we go through the process of giving up caretaking, we place more value on our own lives. The result is enhanced self-esteem.

Making Progress

Now that the words *codependency* and *caretaking* are in our vocabulary, Rachel and I can talk about our behavior in these terms. When she says, "Will you wake me from my nap?" I can say, "No, I think that would be codependent for me to do that today." When she becomes sad and angry and upset because of something that happened to somebody else, we can talk about the pain and then say it's time to move on. For example, she was upsct because she saw a teenage boy intentionally run down a cat and kill it with his car. After an hour of tears, I said, "Let's not dwell on it." That was my mother's phrase, but she'd say it *before* I had cried. For years, I didn't set a limit on the expression of pain—now it's time to limit the energy we give to the pain in the world. It's there but it doesn't have to run or ruin our lives. "Let's experience it, but let's not dwell on it."

One last comment about caretaking: Caretaking as a way of life is extremely stressful to our emotional and physical health. People who are caretaking too much put themselves at risk for addiction and other compulsive behaviors, as well as for such stress-related physical ailments as headaches, digestive tract problems, backaches, and even heart trouble. If your child seems to be a caretaker, you need to know that he or she is susceptible to eating disorders, workaholism, and chemical dependency, in addition to suicidal depression. One of the patterns of caretakers who come from alcoholic families is to develop an eating disorder, either anorexia or compulsive overeating. This is something for you to be aware of.

The good news about clusters of negative behaviors is this: When we work on letting go of caretaking, we release the fuel for many destructive patterns and make progress in many areas at once. Caring about our own well-being brings health to our daily lives and to our relationships.

21

Fast Cars and Designer Jeans: Gender Pressures

> I have to have those shoes and
> designer jeans or nobody will go
> out with me.
> —TROY B.

As our children work out their adolescent crises surrounding sexuality, mortality, and spirituality, sexuality and gender roles may be the most problematic. The adult culture at large doesn't provide many positive images of happy sexuality. Often sexuality is presented as a privilege enjoyed only by people who fit the extreme roles of the masculine and feminine. The media displays exaggerated roles for men and women: skinny blond women and big-muscled men. The media images of a real man and a real woman are virtually impossible to achieve. The great majority of us simply don't fit that ideal male and female in our genetic and physical predispositions. These standards put our kids in a pressure cooker. Sometimes when they try out adult behaviors, they suffer disastrous consequences for their experimentation.

It seems adults are in adamant denial about the true condition of our children. Suicide is only one manifestation of adolescents in pain, adolescents who have not found support, guidance, or a path through the maze of the craziness of contemporary life.

What can we do? Both mothers and fathers need to affirm their children's blossoming individuality. Think about gender roles and support your children if their interests and likes don't fit into socially approved roles. In the book *Growing Up Free: Raising Your Child in the 80's*, Letty Cottin Pogrebin offers many suggestions for ways to support your children to be individuals, rather than people stuffed into a gender role. Her book goes far beyond the general ideas that it's okay for boys to cry and girls to play softball. She has many practical suggestions for raising kids to be free to reach their full potential as people.

As parents, we also need to affirm a healthy sexuality. As our children become mature, we need to affirm their attractive qualities. Take the time to support them in their attempts to look grown-up. Talk about the need to be an individual and the need to fit in with the crowd. Do not ridicule their attempts to look grown-up. Do not ridicule their desire to date and fit in. Help them learn how to be safe and yet have fun. Talk about safe sex, safety on the streets, safety in relationships.

Young women and young men experience different kinds of consequences from these exaggerated gender roles, but both experience difficulty fitting narrowly defined roles.

Being a Young Woman

In spite of the successes of the women's movement, young women have a difficult time finding their identity in today's culture. Women have gained more rights, yet there are still disturbing things going on: more violence against women, increasing images of women being abused and murdered in movies and on television, more emphasis on looking seductive. We mothers gave up our girdles and bras only to find our daughters dieting to fit into men's jeans.

A recent study in Minnesota found that 18 percent of adolescent females contemplate suicide.[1] Related problems they are experiencing include poor body image, eating disorders, depression, and low self-esteem. I told Rachel about the study and the figure of 18 percent didn't surprise her at all. She said, "They needed a study to figure that out?"

The desire to fit in often puts pressures on girls to be sexually active. In the following memoir selection by writer Mary B. Kahle, the adult woman describes the experience of the girl she was at age fourteen.

I.

Glen and David show up at my house one evening. These guys are cool, the most popular freaks in the ninth grade. I am surprised, no, shocked to find them at my door. I act casual. They want me, it seems, to go with them to the carnival. "Ever ride a Ferris wheel on acid?" they grin. "It'll be fun."

Hours and too-bright lights later, dazed and empty-headed, I find myself in David's basement, drinking beer with his older brother. He is big, surly, wearing a black leather jacket. I have heard enough about him to be afraid, but I still act casual, trying to stop the sound of blood that pounds in my ears. Then his hands grip my shoulders, and suddenly, fear is an electric eel that I hold in my mouth. At fourteen, I don't even know enough to call it rape.

I walk home in the darkest of darks. What I want. . . what I long for, is a mother's soft lap, hands stroking my hair, comfort whispered there. A rocking-chair mother, big enough to take me in.

II.

I learned about sex on my own, in secret—about my almost-woman's body, about a cycle more mysterious and mechanical than my new ten-speed bike—from a copy of *Our Bodies, Our Selves* stolen from my school library. I had learned enough to know I could be pregnant.

I tell my mother about what happened the next morning as we sit in the car, in the driveway, in the sun. I want her to help me, to take care of me, because there is something unraveling, unzipping inside of me that I can't name. Her white knuckles grip the steering wheel and she cries, wringing those white hands together, "Oh no, what will we do?" I am slowly becoming wooden.

My sawdust voice tells her my plan, carefully constructed with the phone crisis worker last night while everyone slept, it seemed, but me and that strange woman. She was fantastic to me, the first adult who ever spoke a word about sex to me. Her voice is calm, steady, explaining to me a thing called "the morning after" pill, giving me the names of doctors progressive enough to prescribe it.

The doctor examines me, writes a prescription—four pills, one for each of the next four days. "They'll make you pretty sick," he warns me. Then, "I can give you a prescription for birth control pills, too. . . ."

"No, thank you," I answer primly, as if being passed a tray of cookies at a tea party, "No, I don't think so." A week later I walk the school hallway with wooden legs. Glen and David don't speak to me, but their eyes are amused, knowing. I wonder what they know, and I am marked, branded. I want to slink away, not even a mother would take me in now. Do they know that I spent four days retching in bed, a burning liquid moving snake-like up my throat? That I lay doubled over with cramping, my arms wrapped around myself, while I listened to my mother stay busier than usual in the kitchen, thumping pans around? What I know is that I can't feel any more and that my tears are nothing more than chips of ice. What I know is something I can't understand, but I will live out the lesson in this body of wood, not fit for building or burning.

—Mary B. Kahle

Being a Young Man

The irony of adolescent suicide is that males typically don't show as much depression as females do, yet they kill themselves more often. They also have a high rate of fatal car accidents, often considered hidden suicides. Young African American men and other minority men have a very high homicide rate, which reflects their despair about fitting into the white world. This homicidal behavior might also be construed as hidden suicide.

Nobody really knows why more boys kill themselves than girls. One reason may be that more boys have been trained in the use of weapons and have easier access to them, so they have the means available when there is a motive and opportunity. Whatever the reason, parents of suicidal boys must take precautions with the weapons in the house. Take the warning seriously.

I've learned that my daughter becomes suicidal when she feels that there's no way out, when she's gotten herself in a double bind and can't express the anger. *Double bind* is a psychology term for "being caught between a rock and a hard place." I think something like a double bind is experienced by young men who feel a heavy pressure not to show their feelings in order to fit into the macho role. This is a double bind because they do have feelings. Feeling down and blue is not macho. Boys need as much help as girls in learning how to express their feelings and value their true selves.

In the following journal entry, a man reflects on the pressure on young men to fit the macho role, to be sexual, even if it goes against other feelings:

> It is 1964, and I am sitting in the back seat of a rusted, '56 Ford. Mickey is driving the car down Euclid Avenue, the red light district, and Frank is sitting in front with his arm cocked out the open window. They are two years older, initiating me into the world of sex and prostitution. Frank passes around a can of Stroh's beer. They urge me to relax, but I'm scared and stare out the window.
>
> Finally, Mickey passes a woman he likes, hollers, "That one," and circles around the block until we pull up to the curb behind her.
>
> The woman approaches. She wears a short red miniskirt and her blouse is unbuttoned enough to see that she's braless as she leans over to look

inside the car. "Shove over boy," she says to Frank as she opens the car door and scoots in.

After a few blocks, I sit up and cross my arms over the front seat. I'm curious if she, too, is afraid, how can she be sure she'll get paid. When I ask, she reaches down to the floor as if she dropped a dime, then swirls up the point of a letter opener underneath my chin. "That's how," she says emphatically. I lift my chin up off its point.

"Jesus!" Mickey shouts. "Sit back and relax." I'm trying and look out the window.

The prostitute directs us to a gravel parking lot between two apartment buildings, and tells Frank and me to get out. I do exactly as I'm told and walk across the lot with Frank to stand against the wall of the other building. All I can see is Mickey's head above the front seat of the car. Someone peeks out from behind a curtain in one of the windows on the second floor apartment building.

Mickey comes out of the car in five minutes, grinning, buckling his trousers. . . . . It's my turn. I feel sick to my stomach.

The car door is already opened and I hesitate. "Come on," she says and tells me to swing one leg over her as she hikes up her skirt. I can hardly find the right position and depend on her entirely to tell me what to do. Her eye shadow is smeared. I smell whiskey on her breath. She yanks at my belt, unzips my pants. This isn't the way I want it. She's soaking with sperm. I think I'm suppose to kiss, but there isn't any room here for feelings.

Suddenly, without warning, a spasm shoots through my shoulders, and I'm gagging and retching. "Christ, all mighty," she hollers and pushes me off her. I nearly tumble out of the car onto the gravel.

A tall, muscular man suddenly appears. I don't know where he came from, but he is about to grab me by my shirt collar. "It's okay, the asshole threw up," she says. Really I didn't, I held the vomit in my mouth, then swallowed it. By the time we drive back home, it's dark. Mickey and Frank say nothing to me.

—RICHARD SOLLY

We need to be available to our children as resources when their first adult experiences result in disastrous consequences. When our children hide disasters such as the two described in this chapter, the damage lasts for years.

Part Four

Facing Difficult Life Situations

God wants you, Rachel, to
be the most Rachel you can
be, to be whole, to be as
much as you can be.
—Don Portwood

As you and your child work on your family issues, you will have looked at issues of possible addiction and abuse. In therapy, your child will have looked at issues of loss, stress, depression, anger, and care-taking—all the issues we just discussed. Let yourself consider these pieces of the puzzle one at a time.

After you have made sure your child is safe, there are many different ways to work on the various issues. Don't worry about whether you have chosen the right way to deal with them. Even with professional guidance, you can't look at everything at once. Just keep in mind the factors to be considered. It's okay to skip around in this book. It's sometimes repetitive, because it may be used by different people in a varying sequence of chapters.

After you've worked on the family issues, school problems, and all the feelings we looked at in the last section, it's time to consider certain situations that put great pressure on adolescents. They don't apply to all kids, but when they are present, they greatly intensify the stress level. They have been considered risk factors with suicidal kids. It would be a good idea to be open to all of these possibilities as factors. Let yourself consider each one honestly:

• *Divorce*
• *Sexual Preference*
• *Adoption*
• *Birth Trauma*

22

The Two Fires: Divorce

> She drew an alarming picture of
> someone caught between two
> fires. Someone in the corner is
> calling the fire department and
> saying, "There's a child inside."
> —BERNIE SCHEMMLER

Divorce is hard on kids. On some level we all know this. Yet divorce is so common now that we may resist thinking about how stressful it is for children. It's difficult to face their widespread pain.

Let's start with the truth—the reality of the pain—then consider what can be done to alleviate some of the suffering.

When I was married in my twenties, I vowed never to stay married if it wasn't working, that I'd never stay in a marriage like my parents. Along with thousands of others of my generation, I thought of divorce as a solution. It meant that I would not repeat the pain of my parents' marriage nor force my child to go through years of watching her parents in misery together. For me divorce was a solution.

The "solution" produced unforeseen problems. Unfortunately, the stress of going back and forth between parents and the loss of the dream of an intact family can be devastating to kids. Divorce may change the economic security of the children; it often brings children into a life of poverty, a life that 20–40 percent of American children live in. Divorce always causes a disruption in children's sense of belonging. Divorce may drain children's energy if they are preoccupied with worry and anxiety about their parents' relationship and well-being. The statistics about the aftereffects are startling:

> Although one in three children are from divorced families, they account for an inordinately high proportion of children in mental-health treatment, in special-education classes. . . . Children of divorce make up an estimated 60 percent of child patients in clinical treatment and 80 percent—in some cases 100 percent—of adolescents in inpatient mental hospital settings.[1]

As a parent who has been divorced, the facts are sobering. But in spite of all those negative consequences, there is no way I could have stayed married. I believe that if I had stayed, Rachel would now be worse off emotionally. She would have continued to witness battering and perhaps become a victim of it herself.

No matter what has happened since that marriage in the way of pain, it is not as bad as what I left. I have to remember that. I have to say that often. I have to give myself credit for getting out, for working and hoping for a better life for her and for me. I have to forgive myself for the pain I've put her through. As a result of my work and her work, Rachel has experienced a manageable home life. We both have a glimmer now of what *manageable home life* means.

If you have also been through divorce, and are reading this chapter with fear for the pain you've caused, please forgive yourself for the choices you made. Give yourself and your children the permission to work through all your feelings about the divorce. Go easy on the self-recriminations.

There are three aspects of divorce we'll look at in this chapter. The first is the need for family members to express and fully feel their feelings. The second is for you as a parent to find ways to decrease the tension between you and your former spouse so that negative feelings don't adversely affect your child. The third is for you to work on acceptance of your own situation, to work through the sadness to see yourself as you are now.

Kids' Feelings about Divorce

Divorce has special problems for adolescents. Even though parents may have split up when the

children were very young and have established
new homes and a sense of belonging for the children, at puberty even very secure children have a
need to reprocess all the feelings about the divorce
and about their mom and dad. So regardless
of when your divorce took place, you need to be
willing to see that your child has the opportunity
to express feelings and find the therapy needed if
the child seems to be blocked.

Children, even those in the same family,
express their feelings in different ways. When the
writer Bernie Schemmler was going through a
divorce, she kept a journal. She was worried about
her kids, because even though there had not been
any of the problems of addiction and abuse in her
marriage, she and the kids were feeling devastated.

Looking back through the journal years later,
she noticed the pain of the children, as well as
the individuality of each child's experience. The
following excerpts are from the year that spanned
the breakup. The first few passages are from the
time when the marriage was in bad shape but had
not yet broken up.

> *December 28:* I feel like my face is in pieces.... We
> are so locked in and the kids are beginning to show
> that. I'm always worried about Kathryn who is a
> barometer of our tension and never ever talks
> about it. Anne talks of little else when she's home
> and things are bad. Michael doesn't hear or see it,
> or if he does, buries it. What is this terrible
> process?

March 29: A difficult day despite resolve. Trouble with the kids now—Michael's inertia, passivity, a mirror of Paul's? Anne's social schedule, home so little, attempts to manipulate between Paul and me. Kathryn's requests for stuff, movies, clothes, magazines, books. She asks for things all the time and sometimes forgets that I've already answered, already said "yes" and asks me again. You could say she's not getting what she needs.

August 7: Anne remembered our anniversary yesterday and Kathryn remembered today. Oh, she cried so hard, my poor fragile Kathryn. It's hard for me to understand today why it was necessary to do this. Kathryn tries to hold us all together. She's always asking what we can all do together. She didn't want to go to the movie this afternoon because she would miss Anne's leaving for Gina's cabin. I hope Anne has a wonderful time. It's her only time away this summer. I wish I were away.

September 2: The first day after Paul left. Things are better today. Last night they were so bad for me and the kids. I understand what the books mean by the off-the-wall stage.

September 20: Swing night. A bad night. I'm washing the kids' clothes before they go to Paul's. They're all running behind in their homework and schedules. Me weeping. It is very hard to let them go. I don't want to do it.

November 1: Then I got so angry with Anne.... She took my best sweater and turtleneck over to Paul's. She either hid them in her jacket or stuffed them in her bookbag. I said I needed it. She said,

"Now?" I left and was furious about her rather elaborate deceit.

February 13: I took Kathryn to see a counselor and I think that went well. I thought it was the right thing to do. She drew an alarming picture of someone caught between two fires. Someone in the corner is calling the fire department and saying, "There's a child inside."

March 16: We celebrated lovely Anne's birthday today.... I talked at the table about how she was as a child. I've been doing that a lot when the kids are here, talking about our family life in the past, how it may not be what they want today, but earlier it was a regular home.

—BERNIE SCHEMMLER

From these brief excerpts, we can see how divorce brings a tremendous amount of pain in a family that was pretty happy—a family that had no history of abuse or addiction. I'd say a normal family but that phrase has become volatile. Let's just say this family had been going along on a pretty regular path. We see also that the three children react in very different ways. We can see Kathryn taking in all the sadness, Michael trying to escape, and Anne acting out aggressively. The mother wisely decided that Kathryn needs to be in therapy. Perhaps later Anne and Michael will choose to go to counseling if their feelings become overwhelmingly painful. As outsiders, we might think that Michael and Anne could benefit from therapy now also, yet the family is progressing in its own style.

To help yourself and your children deal with their feelings, please refer back to the chapter on loss as well as the chapter on anger. Grief and anger are probably the two strongest feelings children feel after a divorce. You may need to spend some time reflecting on how your kids may be feeling about your divorce and how it may be compounding the usual feelings of adolescence.

Decrease the Tension Between You and Your Former Spouse

When I was little, I walked around outside with a salt shaker, testing out the theory that if you shake salt on a bird's tail, you'll catch it. When I first heard the idea of "Decreasing tension with your ex-spouse," it sounded a lot like shaking salt on the bird's tail. I laughed to myself and thought angrily, "This is what I call creative problem-solving. Nobody could get along with my psychotic ex-husband."

If you believe that you ex-spouse is a psychotic, a lunatic, a basket case, you may assume that I believe you absolutely. You wouldn't have gotten divorced if he or she were easy to get along with. You can't change the other person, but what can you do? How about some creative problem-solving. Take a few minutes now and list some things you could do to decrease some of the anger in the relationship. Crazy as it sounds, impossible even, you owe it to your kids to see if you can figure out how to decrease the tension between you and your ex-spouse. This is one of the factors most often identified as significant for children to recover from the loss of divorce. The kids who move on with their lives have parents who have become nonchalant about each other.

The advice columnist Pat Gardner published a very encouraging list called "Some Rights of Kids from Divorced Families."[2] This bill of rights affirms the rights of children to live in homes free of tension, abuse, or constant bickering. It affirms the rights of children to have their own feelings, to love and show affection for each parent without the other punishing them. This kind of life is the birthright of all humans—to live in peace and have our own feelings. Although some situations seem impossible to change, let yourself imagine a change. Let go of wanting to make your ex-spouse the partner you wanted.

Certainly, I'm not advocating letting go of situations where there is child abuse. If there is child abuse going on at the other parent's house, report it immediately to Child Protection. Don't try to do it all by yourself. Don't try to change what you can't change.

Try saying the Serenity Prayer as a way to get in touch with the behaviors that are truly under your control—your behaviors, your anger, your joy in your present life. The Serenity Prayer is *God grant me the serenity to accept the things I cannot change, the courage to change the things I can, and the wisdom to know the difference.*

Here are some other suggestions people have tried.

- Be civil—talk with your ex-spouse as if you are in a business relationship.
- Make arrangements for visitation through a third party at a neutral site.
- Ask someone your ex-spouse respects to be an intermediary.
- Ask for official mediation through the courts.
- Don't make nasty remarks about your ex-spouse in front of your kids.
- Do what you can for your kids without talking about what the other parent should be doing.
- Ask your ex-spouse to go to therapy to discuss the children. Be open to listening to your children talk about the other parent in a way that is supportive without being judgmental. Support your children's feelings about their other parent.

If you can't let go of your anger and rage, you must seek professional help. If three years have gone by and you still get into a rage over your ex-spouse, you must get help or your children will be hurt. When you feel angry, ask yourself, "Is hanging on to my anger more important than my child's life?" If you want your child to live, you must do your own work about letting go of your divorce.

To defuse immediate situations that stir up anger in your heart, you might try some of the mottoes that AA and Al-Anon offer. Saying out loud, over and over, "This too will pass," helps dispel the immediate rage, fear, or anxiety at the other parent's behaviors.

For me, one motto wasn't ever enough. So one of my friends who works a Twelve Step program suggests saying five in a row, fast. She has written her own mottoes:

So what?
Who cares?
Forget it.
Don't dwell on it.
It'll all work out.
or: *It'll all come out in the wash.*

I have had and still have much anger at my ex-husband. I have also been angry at the courts and at therapists. Three therapists told him he needed to go to counseling due to his physical violence, but the court would not force him to do this. I was angry that I had no support from the system, no protection. I am still angry that the courts don't take battering into account when they award visitation to fathers. I was told I had to be able to prove that he was insane—committable—in order to have visitation denied.

I have been divorced from him for fifteen years. He has never gone to therapy out of his own desire to get healthy, or to deal with the severe physical abuse he experienced in his childhood. He's only gone to therapy for a few sessions when there's been a crisis—when I said I was leaving him and when Rachel was in the hospital. I am still angry that every time he goes to see Rachel I am vulnerable to his potential for violence. I am angry that I have found it necessary to arrange for third party protection for every occasion he has had visitation. Last year a woman was murdered by her ex-husband when she was in the process of dropping off her daughter for court-ordered visitation. So the anger continues to be a part of my life, and it is a feeling I have to consciously release. I choose to let go of the negative feelings I have had and continue to have.

What this has meant for me is that whenever possible I've walked away from potential conflicts. I decided not to go to court to collect the support he has not paid. I choose not to go to court to try to get Rachel's therapy bills paid. Throughout the past five years, I decided to think of the time when she would be eighteen and there would no longer be money between her dad and me. It is dangerous for me to deal with him. Although this decision has made my life more difficult financially, it is safer. I have my life.

I've done enough work on this now that I can state my feelings and opinion to Rachel without blaming her father. I can comment on the reality of the situation. When she worries about college, I say, "Well, the therapist told him he was stingy because he was a doctor driving a Pinto, but maybe he'll come through with some money for you."

Accept Where You Are Now

After a divorce, the lives of both parents change drastically. Commonly, fathers have a terrible time with their feelings of loneliness and abandonment and women have a terrible time economically. In the first year after divorce in the United States, the income of men goes up 43 percent and the income of women goes down 73 percent.[3]

You might pause for a moment and list the consequences of divorce that have been the most difficult for you to accept. Loneliness? Stress? Anger? What things have happened that have surprised you? Perhaps your ex-spouse moved to another state unexpectedly. Perhaps your kids don't want to come and stay at your apartment on Friday nights. Perhaps you're so filled with abandonment you don't want to even think about dating.

I assume you're going to go to therapy if you are overwhelmed by feelings of despair and loss. In addition to counseling, there are some creative ways to deal with where you are now.

- *Accept the loss of your family being together all in one place.* Draw a picture or a map of where you are and where your kids are and then draw a circle around all of you to connect you in your new living spaces. Use geography to imagine a continuing relationship.
- *Accept the failure of your marriage.* Even though therapists want us to say it's not a failure, it sure as hell feels like a failure. *It's okay to fail.*
- *Accept that holidays are changed forever.* You and your kids won't have the same kind of gatherings for birthdays and religious events. Those days are gone. Make some plans for new celebrations.
- *Accept your feelings of abandonment and practice letting them go.* Accept that you feel deprived and abandoned after divorce. If you are feeling poor and deprived and abandoned, make up a motto right now about you as a parent: "My kids are thriving on my love and potato soup." If you are a noncustodial parent and feel left out and abandoned and deprived, make up a motto for

yourself now: "I give my child loving attention through regular visits, phone calls, and notes."

- *Accept the change in your income level.* If it's down, figure out what you can do to accommodate this change. If you are the custodial parent, you probably won't be able to look after the kids and support them financially the way you want them to be supported. Given this situation, you will have to work on accepting the fact that your income is probably lower than you want it to be. You can consider changing your work to bring in more income. You can look for services that will help you with your kids. If you are a woman, you can be accepting of your situation and work as an activist for groups that are trying to get more support and medical benefits for single mothers and children. Acceptance simply means *start where you are.*

More on Money

Facing the lack of money causes terrible upheavals both in your lifestyle and your emotional life. There are actions you can take, even in the midst of being overwhelmed. You can ask for a friend to sit with you and talk over choices. You can look at your situation in terms of short-term and long-term choices.

Some short-term choices people have made include

- Talk about money issues in a support group without feeling ashamed that you're suddenly poor.
- Cut up your credit cards.
- Apply for food stamps without feeling ashamed.
- Ask a friend for a short-term loan.
- Share your living space with another family.
- Affirm the value of the time you spend with your kids versus material possessions.

Long-term choices about income may include

- Stand up for your rights for an equitable divorce settlement for you and the children.
- Find out what services you qualify for to get job training, such as a displaced homemaker program.
- Set goals for a career change.
- Get professional help if you don't know how to manage the money you do have.
- Acknowledge that it's okay to stay at a low income for the time being.

If your income has gone up since the divorce process, whether you are the mother or father, you might think about how you can use the money to make life easier for your kids. But, be cautious, in American culture, kids often equate money and love. They may feel like you don't love them if you don't give them money and things.

Non-custodial parents often say they don't want to pay more child support because their ex-partners use it for themselves, not the kids. Whether or not this is true, I've heard it so often that I take it as Divorce Truth Number Fifty-Six. If you are holding back financial support for your kids due to the fact that your ex-spouse is a big spender, you may be hurting your kids by preventing them from getting the economic resources they need. If you are doing well financially, how can you use money for your children's benefit? How can you give money to be spent in a way that's somewhat under your control? Here are some suggestions.

- Pay for special equipment for sports or music activities.
- Take them shopping and buy necessities like clothing, shoes, and winter coats.
- Set up a trust fund for their education.
- Make sure they have medical coverage.
- When the children come to see you on the weekend, work on their schoolwork with them so you will be able to see what kinds of gifts would encourage their growth.
- Take them regularly on educational trips that the other parent can't afford.
- Send them to camp.
- Send food home with them.

- Offer to drive them to their various activities: therapy, music lessons, Alateen meeting. Some mundane parental activities are a golden opportunity to grow closer.

Whether you are rich, poor, or just getting by, what kids need from a parent is a dependable, predictable, loving presence, and they need a regular schedule when they can count on seeing you. Write down a plan for the next few months of when you will be doing something fun together.

If you don't feel much acceptance of your situation in your heart right now, know that if you will let yourself write out practical ideas for making the best of things *as they are,* you are creating the conditions of acceptance in your consciousness. You can also create acceptance by looking forward to the time when your children are beyond the current crisis. You will have a new, freer relationship with your children when they are adults. You *will* get through this phase of life.

23

Choices: Sexuality And Self-Acceptance

> I would rather have my son be
> gay than dead.
> —David T.

During adolescence, our sexuality emerges from our inner life out into the world, and many adolescents have a hard time dealing with this aspect of their lives. Our culture is still generally homophobic and withholds the information that 10 percent of all people in all cultures are gay and lesbian. Our culture doesn't provide young people with enough information to help them make informed and healthy choices about their sexuality. In particular, homosexuality is one significant part of the spectrum of sexual knowledge that adults are silent about. The pressure on adolescents to act in the socially approved gender roles that we discussed earlier is intensified if they don't feel any attraction to the opposite sex.

Some young people sense that they don't fit into the norm, yet they don't understand that this lack of conformity may mean they have a preference for their own sex. Other people are conscious of being attracted to their own gender in grade school and junior high school. Many lesbians and gay men recall being conscious at an early age of their sexual preference.

Adolescents who are struggling with sexual preference may feel great distress for a long time, especially if they have not been informed about gay and lesbian choices. They may not know who to talk to. They may be afraid to bring the subject up to their parents for fear of rejection.

One of Rachel's friends in treatment continued to be in distress even after a year of working in family therapy and with her own counselor. She said she didn't know what was bothering her. The counselor and her mother wondered if sexuality was the issue. They asked her directly, and she was tremendously relieved. "How did you know?" she asked. They didn't exactly know how they knew, but they knew. All the other possible issues had been explored. Eventually this young woman felt much more at peace even though she and her friends were harassed for being lesbians.

If your child has received a lot of therapy and your family is making progress but your child is still depressed and suicidal, you must consider whether sexual preference is an issue. Therapists who work with suicidal adolescents say that sexual preference is a source of distress for adolescents much more often than realized. In a recent study of gay and bisexual boys and young men, 30 percent had attempted suicide. The percentage is much higher than the average which is already unbelievably high—14 percent of all young people.[1] Half of the gay and bisexual males had tried to kill themselves more than once. As one parent said, "I didn't want my son to be gay because of all the prejudice he will face in life. But I'd rather have him be gay than dead."

If it is difficult for you to talk about sexual preference, then find someone else who can talk about this with your child. There are support groups in every major city for adolescents and their parents. If you live in a small town, you could try to find resources in the nearest city that could give you support. It is crucial for your child's survival for you to be open to his or her sexual orientation.

24

A Puzzle with a Missing Piece: Adoption

> Who do I look like? Why did
> they get rid of me? I'm a
> puzzle with a missing piece.
> —RACHEL

In the sixties when my first husband and I were married, we thought we'd change the world. We wanted to create the happy childhood home we didn't have. We didn't realize we were an imperfect part of the human condition. We saw all the human frailties *out there* and didn't see the flaws within ourselves. We didn't know it was possible to hurt others unintentionally. We thought adoption was a good thing to do, that we were going to be great parents, and that genetics were irrelevant. If our intentions were good, how could anything bad come out of what we did?

One of the most painful moments of my life was hearing the psychologist say to my daughter, "You have had three major losses in your life, which is a lot more than most kids your age. One, you were adopted; two, your parents got divorced; three, you lost your stepfather." But that's the reality. My good intentions resulted in hurt for someone else. Sometimes there is no way to know which of our actions will result in pain.

Children who are adopted often have a hard time in adolescence dealing with their identity and questions about the meaning of life. The issues around adoption have been emotional ones for Rachel since she was ten years old. At that time she wanted to go to court and examine her files. She gets enraged every time she has to fill out medical forms at school and the doctor's office that ask about family medical history. "How do they expect me to know?" she says angrily. Other reactions to her adoption include a deep sense of abandonment, anger at the system that withholds the information, and a burning desire to know "why." Why did her birth parents get rid of her? Why didn't they tell the social workers their medical history? Why has she had so many problems with depression? Why did God give her bad skin and problems with learning and mood swings? Why can't the adoption files be opened at her request? She also wants to know what her birth parents look like, what they're doing now, and whether she has any siblings.

If your child is adopted and having trouble, do what you can to

- Create a sense of belonging.
- Develop and share a spirituality that affirms that every child is a beloved child of the universe.
- Do some networking with other people who are dealing with adoption issues.
- Be honest: tell your child everything you know.
- Be sure you develop a support network that will be there for you when new related issues come up.
- Look for a support group for adopted kids.
- Deal with all the other issues without being too scared.
- Support your child in searching for birth parents.

If you adopted a child from a racial or cultural background different from you own, your child may have an even stronger desire to search than most kids. If you have not done so before, now is the time to help your child connect with other people from the birth parents' culture and race. A living connection with his or her cultural background is necessary for your child's identity.

After a year in therapy, we began a search for Rachel's birth mother. I didn't feel threatened by this search. After all the fear I've had of her hanging herself out of despair, how could I possibly stand in her way? She has a right to know her own history.

Additionally, I think it would be helpful for her to know her medical background. She wanted to know if her mother has had mental health problems. I wondered if learning problems run in the family or if there is a history of suicidal thinking in her family. I wondered whether or not the birth mother drank while she was pregnant because Rachel's mood swings, accident-prone personality, attention deficit disorder, and lack of judgment all seem possibly related to fetal alcohol syndrome or fetal alcohol effect.

Three years after beginning the search, we did locate Rachel's birth mother, Linda. Rachel and her mother had a tearful, heartfelt reunion. I was so relieved to see her find her missing piece. And the truth is liberating. Rachel's mother is very caring and sweet and open. The truth is that her family does have a history of depression and suicide. She gave Rachel up in hopes of her having a better life. And she managed to keep herself alive to be able to tell her this one day. Rachel is more settled and sure of herself now.

Learning the truth about her biological makeup helped Rachel acknowledge her hard work to become healthy. She has been fighting for her mental health with two strikes against her.

My feelings about finding her birth mother were a deep sense of relief and closure. At the same time I was angry that the family history was withheld from Rachel and me by adoption practices. It would have helped us to know about the learning disabilities, alcoholism, depression, and suicide in her background. I felt like I was part of some experiment to check out the genetic link in suicidal families, except I never consented to be part of the study!

In the end, though, I let go of my anger, knowing that every life is filled with mystery. "Shit happens." "Grace happens." In the end, Rachel is alive in spite of the troubles of her biological and adopted families. Knowing that there is suicide in her family enhances her desire to take care of her mental health, to get help when she needs it.

25

Waters Closing Over: Birth Secrets

> An unacknowledged trauma is like a wound that never heals over and may start to bleed again at any time. In a supportive environment the wound can become visible and finally heal completely.
> —ALICE MILLER

Other parents with suicidal children have told me that some suicidal adolescents have had a trauma at birth or early in life, such as a difficult delivery or parents who were called away for an extended period. These kids are not quite sure if they are supposed to be alive. They are very fragile, and they face the world tentatively. They cling to their home and parents because they're not sure they're supposed to be out there, on their own. They are both fragile and overly dependent.

If this scenario rings true for you, let your child's therapist know because the child will not have any memory of what happened. As parents, we all have important data in our brains, we just don't know which bits are important.

A therapist can help a person work through early, unremembered trauma better than a parent. As parents we feel so much guilt that we have caused pain in spite of our good intentions that it is difficult for us to listen to our children express their pain. I felt guilty that adoption caused Rachel pain. Parents who have had to leave an infant because of work, military service, or other adult emergencies do so without intending to cause lasting damage to their child. It may be very difficult to later look at the damage. That's why I'm saying that if you sense something happened in the first year of life that may have emotionally scarred your child, tell the therapist about your insight. The information may be of help.

When Rachel was born, her birth mother was not allowed to hold her. Rachel was brought to me four days later. Who held her, cuddled her, talked to her in those first four days of life, those long first hours out of the safety of her mother's body? "Who held our baby in the hospital?" both Linda and I ask. We cried together about this deprivation of mothering.

I consider those four days a primary abandonment of our child, set up by a social system that neglects basic human needs for touch, talk, sun, rocking.

When Linda and Rachel met at the airport, they hugged each other with eighteen years of longing that nobody else could have provided. That mother-hug gave Rachel back a vital, physical connection. What we both have given her is knowledge that she was a "wanted" baby.

With the help of the wonderful book *Growing Up Again,* I have also given Rachel other evidence of being wanted: backrubs, healthy touching, and a safe home. "I am glad you were born" is what we all long to hear.

Part Five

Accepting Recovery As A Reality

Eventually, and often after the survival of a long and profound crisis . . . comes the realization that the world is essentially neutral. This discovery can come as a relief, because it is no longer necessary to spend so much energy shoring up the self, and because the world emerges as a broader, more interesting, sweeter place through which to move....

—Frank Conroy

26

A New Picture: Creating A Manageable Family Life

> Treatment has released your
> child to be what God intended:
> a wonderful, energetic teenager
> who wants to test your limits.
> —Sue G.

After a crisis has subsided, life is sweet. How peaceful is the drive to work, the radio playing old favorite songs. How delicious is the coffee in the paper cup. How beautiful is the morning sun, rising red through the smog over the freeway, when the child once at risk is now safe and at peace.

Even as we pause to take in the change, we know life is not problem-free. Peace is a lull, a breather. Life is change, growth, and momentum, and these conditions always embody problems and problem-solving. We can't have muscles without exercise. We can't have mental health without stretching.

Our children will continue to give us problems because that's their job. Their process of growing requires them to test our limits as they stretch and define life on their terms.

Life Can Be Manageable Even with Problems

One of the barriers to my own peace of mind used to be the false belief that life is supposed to be problem-free. It is such a relief to believe that it's okay to have problems. Nobody's perfect. No family is problem-free. In fact, I would shudder at the thought of meeting a family who announces itself to be problem-free.

Now I practice saying, *I have problems and I have the skills to solve them, or live with them, or let them go.* I am inspired by the memory of Gilda Radner, one of my favorite comedians, who took the old cliché "It's always something," and turned it into a title for the book that described her struggle with cancer. All of us have struggles. We can look to other people's inspirational struggles to give us courage to meet our own.

Axioms for Sane Living

Accepting that life comes with problems has been a great boost to my sanity. I stay conscious of other beliefs that I have come to accept. Here are some of them.

- Life is not fair.
- I get to have limits to what I will do for others.
- I won't die from my feelings.
- I get to set limits with everyone, even a suicidal child.
- Families are for continuity, not perfection.
- There are many right ways to live, not just one.
- Money is not proof of self-worth.
- I can learn to relax and have fun.
- I can feel good about myself as a single mother.
- I don't have to be in a relationship to feel good about myself.
- Our kids aren't "done" at age eighteen.

Changing my beliefs about the nature of reality has contributed to having a manageable family life. I encourage you to look at your belief system and notice how it's changed and changing. Becoming more conscious of what you believe now and what you used to believe can renew your commitment to change.

Define *Manageable Family Life* for Yourself

During the first few years I was in therapy, I felt very confused about what I was working toward. I didn't know what kind of family life existed other than the painful one I had known for years. I knew I didn't want to be in such terrible pain. But what would be there when the pain was gone? The future was blank, a fog, an empty picture frame.

Gradually I have defined for myself what goes in the picture frame called *family*. The family of my childhood was not manageable. Since I don't know from personal experience what it is, I have developed my definition from talking to therapists, listening to my body sensations, experimenting with schedules, and living and learning through crises and the process of trial and error. I use the word *manageable* instead of the world *normal,* because the latter has become meaningless. Everyone's normal and nobody's normal.

Here are some of my categories that help me create a picture of "Family Life."

1. *Freedom from Abuse*
   In a manageable family life, family members are free from abuse. This is such a basic idea, many may be surprised I've written it down at all. Finding a home free of abuse has been my lifelong struggle, so this will always be my first thought about healthy living.

2. *Freedom from Tension*
   In a manageable home, the house is free from tension most of the time. People are not walking on eggshells, waiting for the other shoe to drop. Family members trust that they have the skills to resolve conflict when it comes up. For example, after Rachel turned eighteen, we had a conflict

about her curfew. But having conflict doesn't mean there's constant tension in the house. She's testing my limits about setting curfew, and I'm standing my ground and staying calm. A tension-free environment also implies that anger is expressed in appropriate ways. It's like a sudden storm that has an ending, not an ominous, threatening storm that never breaks.

3. *Families Show Respect and Empathy for Each Other*

In a healthy family when something goes wrong, people say, "That's too bad" rather than looking for someone to blame. I was shocked when I heard this. You mean there are people who just say, "Oh"? You mean a mother could just say, "I'm sorry you didn't get a C in Shakespeare. That's too bad, you worked hard."

4. *The Grown-Ups Act like Grown-Ups and the Kids Act like Kids*

Comparing humans to animals helps me clarify the role differences of parents and children. The mother bear is not a playful cub. The cubs don't have to be in charge of defending the home territory.

Likewise, in a healthy family people aren't relegated to rigid roles of hero, clown, responsible kid, mascot. The grown-ups take care of their stuff and the kids get to be kids, which means nobody is overburdened and the roles can move and shift and be flexible.

5. Predictability

There is predictability about how things are going to be at home, both in terms of a routine schedule and also a steady emotional level.

The predictable routine includes weekly maintenance, daily schedules, seasonal celebrations. After my struggles of early sobriety, I learned how to have a manageable home life for the first time. One example of this is doing the grocery shopping on the same night each week. Even though we have a schedule, we don't have rigid rules about dinner at the same time every night. Our schedule suits us. We get special family "talking time" when we go to restaurants. The phone doesn't ring there.

We have a great tradition of seasonal celebrations. I love seeing the year go in its circle, moving from summer to Halloween, to Christmas, to all the spring birthdays. I cherish the holidays now because they have been changed so that they suit us, and I've changed so that I can be with people in a real way. Our list of holidays is our own unique list of celebrations, people, spiritual traditions, and family and friends. It belongs to my daughter and me as a family unit and is shared to some extent by my siblings, but not totally. It is shared by some friends, but not all of it. The only group it belongs to fully is my family unit—me and my daughter.

6. *The Family as a Structure Values the Individuals in It*
The family structure exists to serve the people in it, rather than the other way around. How do you know if your family structure is a healthy one? Here are some guidelines: Does the family make decisions together about holidays? Do people have a say in decisions that affect them, like clothing purchases? Can people change their usual roles? Do people feel free to get help and have fun with people outside the family?

A healthy family offers democracy as well as setting limits and boundaries: people have a structure in which they can change the rules and the old messages.

In a healthy family there is a balance between togetherness and separation. The uniqueness of the individuals is affirmed. The need for children to separate, grow up, and move away is affirmed. The family as a continuing support system is affirmed. There are both planned group activities and individual activities. Both individuality and healthy belonging are seen as good.

7. *A Healthy Family Shares in the Joys, Fun, and Problems of Its Members*
   We learn to enjoy ourselves. Our family now plans for sharing and fun, as part of our schedule. We make room in our lives for joy to happen.

   Spirituality is important, too. The purpose of life on earth is to adore God and enjoy God forever. To have good and loving feelings is our purpose.

8. *Continuity*
   Families exist for continuity. As our children grow up, the role of parents of adult children is to be a continuing resource for them.

   Even though our children aren't done growing up at age eighteen, we don't have to feel guilty. Were we done growing at eighteen?

As Rachel continues to live her life, I see my role as balancing several functions. I am here to be a part of a continuing family unit. I am here for her as a resource person. I maintain routines and limits for running the house. I let her solve her own problems. She makes her schedule, within our parameters. She defines the issues she is going to work on. Slowly she is becoming independent.

I have been inspired by a poem by the writer Linda Wing. It inspires me to be a mother who knows how to both nurture and let go. I'd like to close this chapter—and our story—with her poem.

Glide

Thirteen years old, a summer storm building flat
sky clouds. I could see them moving, track them
   with a
finger, I decided barefoot on cold sand that I
had to swim across the lake. My mother protested.
She said there would be enough to do in life that
   was hard
without making it up. Thirteen years old,
changing into my swim suit, she
took butter off a plate on the table,
told me about English Channel swimmers, that oil
   next to
the skin would keep me warm. She buttered me;
said it would matter when I got to the middle, and
both bays were distant grey eyes. She said, you
don't need to do this. She said, use the sidestroke,
glide when you can.

                    —LINDA WING

Appendix A:
Suicide Warning Signs

The writers of the flyer *Help During a Fragile Time,* suggest that there are four especially serious signals:[1]

1. Threats or talk of killing themselves.
2. Preparing for death evidenced by giving away prized possessions, making a will, writing farewell letters, gathering pills, or saying goodbye.
3. Talking as if there is no hope, even in the future.
4. Acting or talking as if not a single person cares; completely giving up on themselves and others.

Other signs to watch for (those with an asterisk [*] are the most telling signs):

- A change in friends or the amount of time spent with friends.
- Sudden change in behavior.*
- Dramatic change in appetite.
- Sleeping difficulties (and too much sleeping).
- Problems at school.
- Inability to concentrate or sit still.
- Confused thought processes; inability to "think straight."

- Unexplained loss of energy (or wild variations in energy levels).
- Increased drug/alcohol use.*
- Constant feeling of worthlessness or self-hatred (may be covered up).
- Excessive risk-taking (driving recklessly, alcohol use, sex without contraception).*
- Misuse of sex and physical relationships.
- Preoccupation with death, dying, or suicide.*
- Giving away personal or prized possessions.*
- Family history of depression and suicide.

Appendix B:
Your Lifestyle Profile*

Indicate by circling or checking only the signs that apply to you.

The plus (+) and minus (–) signs next to some numbers indicate more than (+) and less than (–).

Exercise

Amount of physical effort expended during the workday: mostly

Heavy physical, walking, housework	Desk work
◯	△

Participation in physical activities, such as skiing, golf, swimming, lawn mowing, gardening?

Daily	Weekly	Seldom
◯	△	☐

Your Lifestyle Profile was developed for community service by the Allstate Insurance Companies and reprinted with their kind permission.

Participation in a vigorous exercise program?

	3 times	
Daily	Weekly	Seldom
○	△	☐

Average miles walked or jogged per day?

| 1+ | −1 | None |
| ○ | △ | ☐ |

Flights of stairs climbed per day?

| 10+ | −10 |
| ○ | △ |

Alcohol

Average number of bottles (12 oz.) of beer per week?

| 0 to 7 | 8 to 15 | 16+ |
| ○ | △ | ☐ |

Average number of hard liquor (1 1/2 oz.) drinks per week?

| 0 to 7 | 8 to 15 | 16+ |
| ○ | △ | ☐ |

Average number of glasses (5 oz.) of wine or cider per week?

0 to 7	8 to 15	16+
○	△	☐

Total number of drinks per week, including beer, liquor, and wine?

0 to 7	8 to 15	16+
○	△	☐

Nutrition

Are you overweight?

No	5 to 19 lbs.	20+ lbs.
○	△	☐

Do you eat a wide variety of foods—something from each of the following five groups: (1) meat, fish, poultry, dried legumes, eggs or nuts; (2) milk or milk products; (3) bread or cereals; (4) fruits; (5) vegetables?

Each Day	3 times Weekly
○	△

Drugs

Do you take drugs?

| No | Yes |
| ◯ | ▢ |

Do you consume alcoholic beverages together with certain drugs (tranquilizers, barbiturates, antihistamines or illegal drugs)?

| No | Yes |
| ◯ | ▢ |

Do you use painkillers excessively?

| No | Yes |
| ◯ | ▢ |

Tobacco

Cigarettes smoked per day?

| None | –10 | 10+ |
| ◯ | △ | ▢ |

Cigars smoked per day?

| None | –5 | 5+ |
| ◯ | △ | ▢ |

Pipe tobacco pouches per week?

None	−2	2+
○	△	▢

Personal Health

Do you experience periods of depression?

Seldom	Occasionally	Frequently
○	△	▢

Does anxiety interfere with your daily activities?

No	Occasionally	Frequently
○	△	▢

Do you get enough satisfying sleep?

Yes	No
○	△

Are you aware of the causes and dangers of sexually transmitted diseases?

Yes	No
○	△

Do you conduct regular breast self-examinations? (If not applicable, do not score.)

Monthly	Occasionally
○	△

Road and Water Safety

Mileage per year as driver or passenger?

-10,000   10,000+

○   △

Do you often exceed the speed limit?

No   by 1 mph+   by 20 mph+

○   △   □

Do you wear a seatbelt?

Always   Occasionally   Never

○   △   □

Do you drive a motorcycle, moped, or snowmobile?

No   Yes

○   △

If yes to the above, do you always wear a regulation safety helmet?

Yes   No

○   □

Do you ever drive under the influence of alcohol?

Never   Occasionally

○   □

Do you drive when your ability may be affected by drugs?

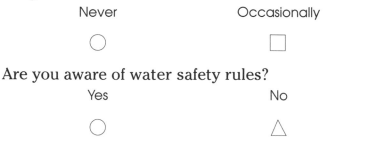

Never   Occasionally
○   □

Are you aware of water safety rules?

Yes   No
○   △

If you participate in water sports or boating, do you wear a life jacket? (If not applicable, do not score.)

Yes   No
○   △

General

Average time watching TV per day (in hours)?

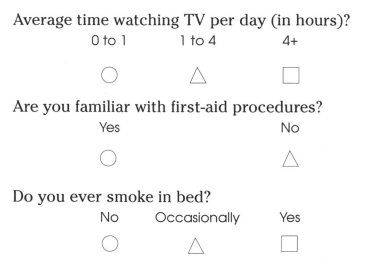

0 to 1   1 to 4   4+
○   △   □

Are you familiar with first-aid procedures?

Yes   No
○   △

Do you ever smoke in bed?

No   Occasionally   Yes
○   △   □

Do you always make use of clothing and equipment provided for your safety at work? (If not applicable, do not score.)

Yes	Occasionally	No
○	△	☐

Scoring Section

Count total number of symbols   ○ △ ☐

1 point for each   ○
3 points for each   △
5 points for each   ☐

Your total score _____

Your Lifestyle Profile will indicate where lifestyle changes should be made, but only if you answer the questions as objectively as possible.

Excellent 34–45: You have a commendable lifestyle based on sensible habits and lively awareness of personal health.

Good 46–55: You have a sound grasp of basic health principles. With a minimum of change you can develop an excellent lifestyle pattern.

Risky 56–65: You are taking unnecessary risks with our health. Several of your lifestyle habits are based on unwise personal choices which should be changed if potential health problems are to be avoided.

Hazardous 66 and over: Either you have little personal awareness of good health habits or you are choosing to ignore them. This is a danger zone—but with a conscientious effort to improve basic living patterns even hazardous lifestyles can be modified and potential health problems overcome.

Appendix C:
How to Tell When Drinking
Is Becoming a Problem*

Alcoholism is a rough word to deal with. Yet nobody is too young (or too old) to have trouble with booze.

That's because alcoholism is an illness. It can hit anyone. Young, old. Rich, poor. Black, white.

And it doesn't matter how long you've been drinking or what you've been drinking. It's what drinking *does to you* that counts.

To help you decide whether you might have a problem with your own drinking, we've prepared these 12 questions. The answers are nobody's business but your own.

If you can answer yes to any *one* of these questions, maybe it's time you took a serious look at what your drinking might be doing to you.

And, if you do need help or if you'd just like to talk to someone about drinking, call us. We're in the phone book under Alcoholics Anonymous.

How to Tell When Drinking Is Becoming a Problem is taken from *A Message to Teenagers . . . How to tell when drinking is becoming a problem,* published by AA World Services, Inc. New York, N.Y. Reprinted with permission of AA World Services, Inc. (See editor's note on copyright page.)

A Simple 12-Question Quiz Designed to Help You Decide

1. Do you drink because you have problems? To relax?
2. Do you drink when you get mad at other people, your friends or parents?
3. Do you prefer to drink alone, rather than with others?
4. Are your grades starting to slip? Are you goofing off on your job?
5. Did you ever try to stop drinking or drink less—and fail?
6. Have you begun to drink in the morning, before school or work?
7. Do you gulp your drinks?
8. Do you ever have loss of memory due to your drinking?
9. Do you lie about your drinking?
10. Do you ever get into trouble when you're drinking?
11. Do you get drunk when you drink, even when you don't mean to?
12. Do you think it's cool to be able to hold your liquor?

Endnotes

Introduction
1. *USA Today,* 5 December 1988, 22.
2. Brent Q. Hafen and Kathryn J. Frandsen, *Youth Suicide: Depression and Loneliness* (Boulder, Colo.: Cordillera Press, 1986), 11.

Chapter 1
1. Adapted from Ann Landers, Minneapolis *Star Tribune,* 24 September 1988, and *Help During a Fragile Time,* a flyer from the Extension Service of the University of Minnesota, 4H-FS-3081, 1986.

Chapter 3
1. Paul G. Quinnett, *Suicide: The Forever Decision* (New York: Continuum, 1987), 1. I recommend reading the whole book in order to learn how to talk about suicide calmly. It is the best book I've found.

Chapter 8
1. Arthur Applebee, *A Study of Book-Length Works Taught in High School English Courses* (Albany, N.Y.: Center for the Study of Teaching and Learning of Literature, 1989).

Chapter 10
1. Ellen Bass and Laura Davis, *The Courage to Heal* (New York: HarperCollins, 1988), 202.

Chapter 11

1. NIAAA Research Monograph 4, *Services for Children of Alcoholics,* DHHS Pub. No. ADM 81-1007 (Washington, D.C.: GPO, 1981).

2. The National Woman Abuse Prevention Project, *Effects of Domestic Violence on Children and Domestic Violence Fact Sheet,* Washington, D.C.: The National Woman Abuse Prevention Project.

3. Brent Q. Hafen and Kathryn J. Frandsen, *Youth Suicide: Depression and Loneliness* (Boulder, Colo.: Cordillera Press, 1986), 67.

4. Stephen Farmer, M.A., M.F.C.C., *Adult Children of Abusive Parents* (New York: Ballantine, 1990).

5. Meister Eckhart, quoted in Matthew Fox, *Original Blessing* (Santa Fe: Bear & Co., 1983), 277.

Chapter 12

1. Tony A. and Dan F., *The Laundry List: The ACOA Experience* (Deerfield Beach, Fla.: Health Communications, 1991).

Chapter 15

1. Patricia Hersche, "The Resounding Silence," *Networker,* July/August 1990.

Chapter 16

1. Richard Obershaw, "Grief Counseling/Therapy," *The Phoenix,* December 1989, 8.

2. John W. James and Frank Cherry, *The Grief Recovery Handbook* (New York: Harper & Row, 1988).

Chapter 17

1. David Elkind, *The Hurried Child: Growing Up Too Fast Too Soon* (Redding, Mass: Addison-Wesley, 1981).

Chapter 19

1. William Styron, *Darkness Visible: A Memoir of Madness* (New York: Random House, 1990). This book can be useful for background material.

Chapter 21

1. Survey conducted by Minnesota Department of Education, as reported in Minneapolis *Star Tribune*, 15 September 1992, 1A.

Chapter 22

1. Judith S. Wallerstein, "Children After Divorce: Wounds That Don't Heal," *New York Times Magazine*, 22 January 1989. This article describes her research published in *Second Chances: Men, Women & Children a Decade after Divorce* (New York: Ticknor & Fields, 1989).

2. Pat Gardner, "Children's bill of rights promote dialogue in families of divorced," Minneapolis *Star Tribune*, 5 July 1989, 10E.

3. L. J. Weitzman, *The Divorce Revolution: The Unexpected Social and Economic Consequences for Women and Children in America* (New York: Free Press, 1985).

Chapter 23

1. Lewis Cope, "Many young gays say they tried suicide," Minneapolis *Star Tribune*, 31 May 1991, 5BW.

Appendix A

1. *Help During a Fragile Time,* a flyer from the Extension Service of the University of Minnesota, 4H-FS-3081, 1986.

Recommended Reading

A., Tony, and Dan F. *The Laundry List: The ACOA Experience.* Deerfield Beach, Fla.: Health Communications, 1991.

Bass, Ellen, and Laura Davis. *The Courage to Heal: A Guide for Women Survivors of Child Sexual Abuse.* New York: HarperCollins, 1988.

Beattie, Melody. *Codependent No More.* New York: Harper & Row, 1987.

Burns, David D. *Feeling Good: The New Mood Therapy.* New York: NAL Dutton, 1981.

Clarke, Jean Illsley, and Connie Dawson. *Growing Up Again: Parenting Ourselves, Parenting Our Children.* Center City, Minn.: Hazelden Educational Materials, 1989.

Davis, Martha, Elizabeth R. Eshelman, and Matthew McKay. *The Relaxation and Stress Reduction Workbook.* Oakland, Calif.: New Harbinger Publications, 1988.

Fossum, Merle, and Marilyn Mason. *Facing Shame: Families in Recovery.* New York: Norton, 1986.

Hafen, Brent Q., and Kathryn J. Frandsen. *Youth Suicide: Depression and Loneliness.* Boulder, Colo.: Cordillera Press, 1986.

Mahdi, Louise Carns, Steven Foster, and Meredith Little, eds. *Betwixt & Between: Patterns of Masculine and Feminine Initiation.* LaSalle, Ill.: Open Court Publishing, 1987.

Mariechild, Diane. *Inner Dance: A Guide to Spiritual and Psychological Unfolding.* Freedom, Calif.: Crossing Press, 1987.

Miller, Alice. *Thou Shalt Not Be Aware: Society's Betrayal of the Child.* New York: Farrar, Straus & Giroux, 1984.

Recommended Reading

NiCarthy, Ginny. *Getting Free: A Handbook for Women in Abusive Relationships.* Seattle: The Seal Press, 1962.

Pogrebin, Letty Cottin. *Growing Up Free: Raising Your Child in the 80's.* New York: McGraw Hill, 1980.

Quinnett, Paul G. *Suicide: The Forever Decision.* New York: Continuum, 1987.

Rosellini, Gayle, and Mark Worden. *Here Comes the Sun: Finding Your Way Out of Depression.* New York: Harper/Hazelden, 1987.

Viorst, Judith. *The Tenth Good Thing about Barney.* New York: Macmillan, 1971.

Index

Other titles of interest...

Growing Up Again
Parenting Ourselves, Parenting Our Children
by Jean Illsley Clarke and Connie Dawson
Growing Up Again helps parents find a course through the child-rearing years by providing detailed explanations on the difference between love and indulgence, structure and criticism, and independence and abandonment. Personal stories, examples, charts, and suggested activities help parents identify normal and dysfunctional childhood experiences. 188 pp.
Order No. 5063

The Promise of a New Day
by Karen Casey and Martha Vanceburg
This daily guide reaches out to all of us who seek full, healthy living. One page at a time, one day at a time, these meditations guide our path, affirm our strength, and give us a sense of hope and peace. *The Promise of a New Day* is a supportive resource for men and women looking for greater rewards in daily life. 400 pp.
Order No. 1045

Dancing Backwards in High Heels
How Women Master the Art of Resilience
by Patricia O'Gorman
A positive, practical guide to understanding resilience and its role in everyday life, *Dancing Backwards in High Heels* examines areas of discontent and conflict for women and demonstrates how we can resume control over our lives, make better choices, and enhance our ability to meet our goals and priorities. 184 pp.
Order No. 1494

For price and order information, or a free catalog, please call our Telephone Representatives.

HAZELDEN

1-800-328-0098   **1-612-257-4010**   **1-612-257-1331**
(Toll-Free. U.S., Canada,   (Outside the U.S.   (24-Hour FAX)
and the Virgin Islands)   and Canada)

Pleasant Valley Road • P.O. Box 176 • Center City, MN 55012-0176